HARLEM HOLIDAY / The Harlem Plug

The Harlem Plug

THE RICHARD 'FRITZ' SIMMONS STORY

HARLEM HOLIDAY

New York, New York
Copyright © 2021 Harlem Holiday

Without limiting the rights under copyright reserved above, no part of this publication maybe reproduced, stored in or introduced into retrieval system, or transmitted, in any form or by any means (electronic, mechanical, photocopying, recording or otherwise), without the prior written permission of the copyright owner.

Edited by, Carol Taylor, Brown Sugar Books
Copyedited by, Nira A. Hyman, Hyman Publishing
Cover Designed by, Najdan Mancic
Cover Model: Richard Allen Simmons a.k.a. Fritz

All photographs courtesy of the author unless otherwise indicated.

This is a work of nonfiction compiled using numerous interviews, of the people in their life at that time, news clippings and trial transcripts. Although this story has been told many years later, the people, incidents and dialogue are real, and are as accurate as the Simmons and Harrison Family's memory of them, and the numerous people interviewed can be. It is important to note, that some of the names have been changed for various reasons.

The scanning, uploading, and distribution of this book via the internet or via any other means without the permission of the publisher is illegal and punishable by law. Please purchase only authorized electronic editions and do not participate in or encourage electronic piracy of copyright materials. Your support of the author's rights is appreciated.

ISBN 978-0-9906131-1-4

Printed in the United States of America
For more information, visit HarlemWestsidePublishing.com

THIS BOOK IS DEDICATED TO THE
SIMMONS & HARRISON FAMILY RICHARD
ALLEN SIMMONS aka "FRITZ"

SUSANNA SIMMONS
Mother of Richard Allen Simmons

CLIFFORD HARRISON
Father of Richard Allen Simmons and Sheila Harrison

EVELYN SIMMONS & SHEILA HARRISON
Sisters of Richard Allen Simmons

DOMINIQUE J. SIMMONS, SEQUOYAH M. SIMMONS,
CHANCE A. SIMMONS, RICHARD A. SIMMONS,
RAYMOND D. SIMMONS, TERRY SIMMONS, MANDY
WILLIAMS, AND ERIN A. CUNNINGHAM
The Children of Richard Allen Simmons

SAUNDRA SIMMONS (R.I.P)
Daughter of Evelyn and Niece of Richard Allen Simmons

ELIZABETH & CLAUDE ROBINSON
Sheila Harrison's Grandparents

CLIFFORD "JUNIOR" HARRISON and
GERVASE "TYRAY" WALKER
Richard Allen Simmons' Half-brothers

NICOLE M. ASHBROURE, RAVEN G. HARRISSON,
NEIL R. HARRISON, AND HOWARD T. HARRISON
Children of Sheila and Richard Allen Simmons' Nieces and Nephews

AUTHOR'S NOTE

The Richard Allen Simmons' story is bigger than the money he made from the game, or his accolades as a Harlem street legend and New York City's most respected and under-the-radar cocaine consignment kingpin of the '80s and early '90s. It's a story about Richard Allen Simmons, known in the drug game as 112th Street Fritz. It's the untold history that shaped his life from beginning to end, the monsters that tore Fritz's family apart, and their survival in the belly of the beast over three decades.

My name is Tiffany Símone Fulton. I was born and raised in Harlem, and now write under the pen name HARLEM HOLIDAY. Like the famous jazz singer, Billie Holiday, I acquired the signature flower above my ear, a style that symbolizes sophistication, glamour, and femininity.

I came from a middle-class family, raised in a single-parent household by a mother who wanted the best for her daughter and sent me off to Oakwood Friends School, a boarding school in Poughkeepsie, New York. I was often called Miss goody-two-'shoes or white girl. Yes, I was a good-girl that liked bad-boys. I knew and dated some of the major players in the drug game in Harlem, but I wasn't in the street. I met many of these bad boys through acquaintances, at parties, or on the bus ride social get-togethers my friend, Darold "D Ferg" Ferguson (R.I.P) gave. He was a Harlem Boutique shop owner who designed the now iconic Bad Boy record label logo.

I never had the opportunity to personally meet Fritz but I was introduced to the infamous Harlem street legend turned government witness, Alpo Martinez. I had a brief encounter with Azie Faison who's story became a Hollywood hood classic, *Paid-In-Full*, produced by Damon Dash and Roc-A-Fella films.

I met Sheila Harrison, Fritz's sister through her husband Russell. His dogs, Diva and Munch would mark their territory every morning at the front of my flea market/farmers market on the corner of 8th Avenue and 117th Street in Harlem. A few months later Sheila lost her grandmother. I gave her a job at my market, brought her into my very busy world hoping to keep her mind off her loss. We developed a close bond and sisterhood. In 2014, I had just completed my first book, *Fallen Petals: The Deception, The Deceit, and The Damned* when she asked me to write this story, to set the record straight for all Harlemites and any fan of Harlem's history. This book is for avid readers of crime nonfiction, incorporated with a side not normally added in such books. It's a look inside the lives of the gangsters, kingpins, money-makers, and shakers that controlled the drug trade in Harlem during that time.

My journey in writing *The Harlem Plug* was an emotional roller-coaster ride, but worth the time and energy it took to bring you Fritz's story. It's a Shakespearean tragedy set in the hood that will pull you deeper into his world with every page.

Enjoy the ride,
Harlem Holiday

"You are the light of the world. A city set on a hill cannot be hidden. Nor do people light a lamp and put it under a basket, but on a stand, and it gives light to all in the house. In the same way, let your light shine before others, so that they may see your good works and give glory to your Father who is in Heaven."

—**Matthew** 5:14-16

ACKNOWLEDGEMENTS

Thank you Darrell, my husband and best friend, for all your help, insight, patience, and the endless sacrifices you made so I could write this book. Ronnie, my favorite and only son. Love you to the moon and back, Thank you for taking part in my dreams, Words can't truly describe or show how much you both are truly loved, appreciated, and needed.

Thank you Evelyn and Sheila, for trusting your brother's story to me, for believing in me, and having the confidence that I would do Fritz's story justice. Adrian "Ace" Small and family, thank you for opening your doors and your life to me. Erin A. Cunningham, Daughter of Richard 'Fritz' Simmons, for your support in getting your father's story in the hands of many.

MANY THANKS TO:

Kevin & Tiffany Chiles
Don Diva Magazine

Damen Heyward and Jimi Kendix,
"The Harlem Plug" Soundtrack Producers

Ed Shooter
E & E Productions

Eartha Watts Hicks
NYCHA/NAACP Bestselling Author of Love Changes

Carl Michel & Martin Pratt,
Write A Legacy

Richard E. Ashby, Jr.
LiteracyNation Director / BCALA President

Kwame "Dutch" Teague
Essence #1 Bestselling Author of Dutch Trilogy

CONTENTS

Prologue 1

1960s

1. Who That Knocking On My Door? 17
2. The Boogeyman Is Here 25
3. The Boogeyman's Reign Of Fear 36

1970s

4. Before There Was A Fritz 46
5. The Queen Of The Dunbar 53
6. The Boogeyman Under The Bed 68
7. Escape From The Boogeyman 76
8. The Boogeyman Come And Gone 84
9. Harlem Boy Lost 91
10. A Family Reunion 101
11. Death's Toll 110

1980s

12. Rise of the King Of Kingpins 123
13. Black Ice "The Enforcer" 148
14. The Pit 153
15. An Ace In The Hole 157
16. Thirty Silver Coins 167

1990s

17. The Wild Cowboys Dead or Alive 175
18. The Domino Effect Of The Game 187
19. A Turning Point 191
20. Running Out Of Time 200
21. The End 208

Epilogue	214
A Daughter's Love Letter	217
Sheila's Message Of Appreciation	219
Adrian "Ace" Small Brief Case Summary	222
Letters To Heaven	237
About The Author	245
Lost Innocence	251
Find Me	260

PROLOGUE

Harlem's History And Hustlers At A Glance

Although Harlem was first inhabited by Native Americans, the first European settlers in Harlem were the Dutch immigrants in 1637, then the French, English, and a small group of Russians. Harlem became the center of the black cultural revival because of the high rates of migration of blacks from the South to the North, and a cluster of those migrants in a small area in North Manhattan. Harlem's black population increased by 66% between 1910 and 1920. This sharp rise in the number of black tenants was due to the available tenements in the area which were constructed for white tenants. A financial crisis triggered an economic depression and caused Harlem property values to drop by 80%. A delay in the building of the subway from lower Manhattan to Harlem also contributed to a fall in real estate prices.[1] Desperate to save themselves from financial ruin, white landlords were willing to rent properties to blacks regardless of the racist, discriminatory policy in private housing.

---

[1]   Wikipedia contributors, "History of Harlem," Wikipedia, The Free Encyclopedia, https://en.wikipedia.org/w/index. php?title=History_of_Harlem&oldid=922501915 (accessed December 2, 2019)

Philip A. Payton Jr., a porter in a real estate office making $8 per week, got the idea of going into the real estate business on his own, and founded the Afro American Realty Company. He took advantage of the white's financial troubles, bought up property and steered black clients to Harlem. In 1914, *The Outlook*, a weekly magazine published in New York City, wrote that three-quarters of the black population of New York City, including all blacks of prominence, lived in Harlem; it called Philip A. Payton Jr., "the father of his Negro community." The success of Payton's enterprise could be seen in the neighborhood of 13 West 131st Street, the house he had bought for himself and his wife, Maggie, in 1903. The entire street was white in 1900, but according to the New York State census, in 1915, the block was almost completely inhabited by blacks.[2] Top bookies—bankers running the numbers racket in Harlem—like Casper "The Bolito King" Holstein and Stephanie St. Clair, known as "Queen" or Madam St. Clair, also became known as financial powerhouses and invested heavily in Harlem real estate. Wealthier blacks continued to buy land in Harlem until 40% of Harlem's private houses and 10% of its tenements were owned by black people.[3]

Philip A. Payton Jr. became known as the "Father of Harlem," the real estate mogul who turned Harlem into a black mecca.

In the beginning of the 20th century, the first generation of educated free-born African Americans fled to the North due to the rise of the racial hatred in the Southern states and the debates on

---

[2] Wikipedia contributors, "Philip A. Payton Jr.," Wikipedia, The Free Encyclopedia, https://en.wikipedia.org/w/index.php?title=Philip_A._Payton_Jr.&oldid=925107512 (accessed December 2, 2019).

[3] (3a) Wikipedia contributors, "Harlem," Wikipedia, The Free Encyclopedia, https://en.wikipedia.org/w/index.php?title=Harlem&oldid=926038447 (accessed December 2, 2019).

racial inequality. A newfound black pride and solidarity would peak during the 1920s with the Harlem Renaissance, when it became the capital for black entertainers and literary artists including Duke Ellington, Louis Armstrong, Josephine Baker, Langston Hughes, Zora Neale Hurston, Marcus Garvey, and W.E.B. Du Bois. Blacks from the South, the Caribbean, and Africa converged on Harlem during this time bringing with them unique experiences, cultures, and educations to create a one-of-a-kind community. Harlem became the world stage for the "New Negro," and found a white audience that embraced the song and dance they brought with them.[4] Still, they faced segregation in entertainment establishments even within their own community—at the Cotton Club, for example, black artists could perform for the white patrons, but could not sit in the audience. Some blacks operated alternative, private venues in their homes called "buffet flats." The buffet flats offered alcohol, music, dancing, prostitutes, gambling, and rooms for couples. It also offered a degree of privacy from police and from whites.[5]

Harlem was a stronghold of the Italian Mafia, who arrived in the late 19th century and early 20th century. The neighborhood became known as "Italian Harlem," the Italian American hub of Manhattan.[6] There were many crime syndicates in Italian Harlem,

---

[4]   (4a) The Editors of Encyclopedia Britannica, "Harlem race riot of 1964", Encyclopedia Britannica, Inc., https://www. britannica.com/event/Harlem-race-riot-of-1964 (accessed December 02, 2019)

[5]   (3b) Wikipedia contributors, "Harlem," Wikipedia, The Free Encyclopedia, https://en.wikipedia.org/w/index.php?title=Harlem&oldid=926038447 (accessed December 2, 2019).

[6]   Wikipedia contributors, "Giglio Society of East Harlem," Wikipedia, The Free Encyclopedia, https://en.wikipedia. org/w/index.php?title=Giglio_Society_of_East_Harlem&old id=900857599 (accessed December 2, 2019).

from the early Black Hand, an Italian-American extortion racket, to the bigger and more organized Italian gangs that formed the Mafia. It was the founding location of the Genovese crime family, run by Charles "Lucky" Luciano. Lucky was a criminal mastermind, the first official boss of the Genovese crime family and head of the Commission, the governing body of the five families that ran the Mafia.

Black criminals began to organize themselves similarly. A small group of blacks found success outside the law, concentrating on the "policy racket," and the number's game, or *bolita*, in East Harlem. Invented around 1920, "playing the numbers" had exploded by 1924 into a racket turning over tens of millions of dollars every year. That year, *The New York Age*, one of the most influential black newspapers of its time, reported that there were at least thirty bankers, or number runners, in Harlem. During the 1920s and 1930s, black organized crime was centered in Harlem, where the numbers racket was largely controlled by Holstein and Madam St. Clair. Both fought gun battles with Jewish-American mobster Dutch Schultz over control of the lucrative trade.[7]

In 1931, Dutch Schultz tried to assert control over the wealth of Harlem residents with a campaign of violence and blackmail involving banks, restaurants, and clubs. Schultz took advantage of his political and police contacts to launch this attack.[8] When he was killed four years later by Murder Inc. (Murder Incorporated

---

[7] (3c) Wikipedia contributors, "Harlem," Wikipedia, The Free Encyclopedia, https://en.wikipedia.org/w/index.php?title=Harlem&oldid=926038447 (accessed December 2, 2019).

[8] (8a) Wikipedia contributors, "Crime in Harlem," Wikipedia, The Free Encyclopedia, https://en.wikipedia.org/w/index. php?title=Crime_in_Harlem&oldid=916137887 (accessed December 2, 2019).

founded by New York Jewish American mobsters Meyer Lansky and Benjamin "Bugsy" Siegel in the early 1920s and acted as the enforcement arm of the Italian-American Mafia and Jewish mob), Harlem did not weep for him.[9]

The neighborhood declined rapidly once World War II ended. The mid-20th century saw a dramatic increase in organized criminal rackets and the gangsters (i.e. Charles "Lucky" Luciano, Dutch Schultz, Casper Holstein, Madam Saint Claire, Ellsworth Raymond "Bumpy" Johnson, Red Dillard Morrison, Frank Lucas, and Leroy "Nicky" Barnes) of Harlem were among the most notorious in American his-tory.[10] By the early 1950s, the money at play amounted to billions of dollars. The police force had been thoroughly corrupted by bribes from the number's bosses, murder was on the rise, and essentially all white people plus much of the black middle class had left Harlem.[11] It left an opening for the wave of Latinos and Hispanics who immigrated to the United States during this period. Italian Harlem would later be called Spanish Harlem, or *El Barrio*, the term for a Spanish-speaking neighborhood or city.

By the 1960s, Harlem was quickly reeling toward decay. Any city money earmarked for Harlem disappeared during "white flight"—the large-scale departure of white people from urban

---

[9] Wikipedia contributors, "Murder, Inc.," Wikipedia, The Free Encyclopedia, https://en.wikipedia.org/w/index. php?title=Murder,_Inc.&oldid=928342808 (accessed December 2, 2019).

[10] (8b) Wikipedia contributors, "Crime in Harlem," Wikipedia, The Free Encyclopedia, https://en.wikipedia.org/w/index. php?title=Crime_in_Harlem&oldid=916137887 (accessed December 2, 2019).

[11] (3d) Wikipedia contributors, "Harlem," Wikipedia, The Free Encyclopedia, https://en.wikipedia.org/w/index.php?title=Harlem&oldid=926038447 (accessed December 2, 2019).

neighborhoods or schools increasingly populated by minorities.[12] Further, the neighborhood was riddled with crime, poverty, corrupt police, and illicit drugs. The Congress of Racial Equality (CORE), a civil rights organization founded in the 1942 acted as a negotiator for the community with the city, especially in times of racial unrest. CORE urged civilian review boards to hear complaints of police abuse, a demand that was ultimately met. Community relations between Harlem residents and the NYPD were strained as civil rights activists requested that the NYPD hire more black police officers in Harlem. In 1963, Inspector Lloyd Sealy became the first African-American officer of the NYPD to command a police station, the 28th Precinct in Harlem. It was a start.[13]

Despite Black nationalism (a type of political thought that seeks to promote social, political, and economic empowerment of black communities and people, and maintain a distinct black identity), the Civil Rights Act of 1964 (which ended segregation in public places and banned employment discrimination on the basis of race, color, religion, sex or national origin), and the Voting Rights Act of 1965 (a landmark piece of federal legislation in the United States that prohibited racial discrimination in voting), Black folks continued to struggle under the oppression and discrimination of being Black in America.[14] The beginning of lynchings, which

---

[12] (4b) The Editors of Encyclopedia Britannica, "Harlem race riot of 1964", Encyclopedia Britannica, Inc., https://www. britannica.com/event/Harlem-race-riot-of-1964 (accessed December 02, 2019)

[13] (3e) Wikipedia contributors, "Harlem," Wikipedia, The Free Encyclopedia, https://en.wikipedia.org/w/index.php?title=Harlem&oldid=926038447 (accessed December 2, 2019).

[14] History.com Editors. "Civil Rights Movement." History, A&E Television Networks, 27 October 2009, https://www.history.com/topics/black-history/civil-rights-movement.

lead to redlining and gerrymandering, ultimately resulted in the ravishing of drugs in the urban communities. By the '60s, the drug addiction rate in Harlem was ten times higher than the New York City average, and twelve times higher than the United States as a whole. Most New Yorkers were unaware of just how young junkies were becoming until December 16th, 1969, when all the newspaper headlines were about a 12-year-old boy named Walter Vandermeer, found dead of a heroin overdose in a Harlem tenement.[15] At that time there were estimated to be 30,000 drug addicts living in New York City, 15,000 to 20,000 lived in Harlem.

Property crime was widespread, and the murder rate was six times higher than New York's average. Half of the children in Harlem grew up with one parent, or none, and lack of supervision contributed to increased juvenile delinquency. Between 1953 and 1962, the crime rate among young people increased throughout the city but was consistently 50% higher in Harlem than in New York City as a whole due to the influx of drugs.[16]

Across the world, armed servicemen felt the sting of drug addiction as well. Those serving in the Vietnam War used drugs more heavily than any previous generation of enlisted U.S. troops. The April 2018 article by Adam Janos, "G.I.s' Drug Use in Vietnam Soared—With Their Commanders' Help," stated that "substance abuse in the Vietnam War wasn't just limited to the marijuana and heroin enlistees could buy on the black market. Military

---

[15] Lelyveld, Joseph. "Obituary of a Heroin User Who Died at 12." The New York Times, 12 January 1970. https://www. nytimes.com/1970/01/12/archives/obituary-of-a-heroin-user-who-died-at-12-obituary-of-walter.html

[16] (3f) Wikipedia contributors, "Harlem," Wikipedia, The Free Encyclopedia, https://en.wikipedia.org/w/index.php?title=Harlem&oldid=926038447 (accessed December 2, 2019).

commanders also heavily prescribed pills to help improve soldiers' performance. Sedatives were prescribed to help relieve anxiety and prevent mental breakdowns."

From marijuana to amphetamines and heroin, drugs were commonplace among the troops. After an investigative trip overseas in 1970, liaison to the Bureau of Narcotics and Dangerous Drug Egil Krogh told President Richard Nixon, "You don't have a drug problem in Vietnam; you have a condition. Problems are things we can get right on and solve."[17]

The Vietnam War lasted almost 20 years (1955-1975) and included more than 58,000 American casualties; drugs had taken a toll on hundreds of thousands. The government created the addicts and then abandoned them. It left many returning soldiers—particularly black ones—abandoned in ghettos with limited outreach programs to help them sort out their unique mental issues. At the same time, veterans needed to be weaned off all the drugs the government had supplied them freely during the war.

The black vets that fought in Uncle Sam's war returned home facing many issues: racial injustice, few jobs, and families unequipped to handle the unstable, shell-shocked addicts turning up at their doors. Abandoned by the government, disenfranchised, and unable to reconnect to everyday life in America, scores of veterans were left to their own coping mechanisms. The drugs that helped the soldiers survive the war now offered them peace from painful memories and scars Vietnam had left behind.

President Nixon wrote Congress once that New York City alone had records of some 40,000 heroin addicts. In his June 17, 1971, press conference, he declared a "war on drugs," and named

---

[17] Janos, Adam. "G.I.s' Drug Use in Vietnam Soared—With Their Commanders' Help." History, A&E Television Networks, 18 April 2018, https://www.history.com/news/drug-use-in-vietnam

drug abuse as "America's public enemy No. 1."[18] He dramatically increased the size and presence of federal drug control agencies and pushed through measures such as mandatory sentencing and no-knock warrants. (In the United States, a no-knock warrant is a warrant issued by a judge that allows law enforcement officers to enter a property without immediate prior notification to the residents, such as by knocking or ringing a doorbell.)[19]

Heroin affected everyone, white and black—no one was excluded. It affected the poor, the middle class, and the rich. Even though heroin use was prevalent in ghettos, especially in Harlem, suburban whites would risk all to come to Harlem to get heroin, known on the streets as smack.

For example, one humid September evening in 1979, police from Manhattan's 28th Precinct responded to an emergency call from the Shelton Plaza Hotel at 300 West 116th Street. The Shelton was a known shooting gallery in Harlem where IV drug users congregated, purchased, and injected—or, "shot"—heroin. EMTs found David Anthony Kennedy, 24-year-old son of the late senator Robert F. Kennedy, dazed and bruised in the lobby. David told the police he was beaten and robbed, but he eventually confessed to the police: "I'm a stoned-out junkie." Heroin was not picky about its victims.[20]

---

[18] DrugPolicy.org Editors. "A Brief History of the Drug War." We Are the Drug Policy Alliance, http://www.drugpolicy.org/ issues/brief-history-drug-war (accessed December 02, 2019).

[19] Wikipedia contributors, "No-knock warrant," Wikipedia, The Free Encyclopedia, https://en.wikipedia.org/w/index. php? title=No-knock_warrant&oldid=918024474 (accessed December 2, 2019).

[20] "2 in Harlem Rob David Kennedy, 24-Year-Old Son of Late Senator." The New York Times Archives, 6 September 1979, Section D, Page 21 https://www.nytimes.com/1979/09/06/archives/2-in-harlem-rob-david-kennedy-24yearold-son-of-late-senator.html?login=email&auth=login-email

The heroin scene was the beginning of the end of Harlem, a downward spiral into the abyss. In Harlem, zombie-like, strung-out addicts roamed the streets, scratching compulsively and nodding off. They wrapped their sores and track marks in bandages to cover up evidence of gangrene and pus-infected limbs.

A Harlem heroin addict nicknamed Claw had a hand swollen 10 times its normal size. It was also covered in maggots and infected so badly by heroin use, many on the streets that came in contact with Claw said, he smelled like death. It was said by a council member in Nicky Barnes' (a notorious heroin kingpin of the 1970s Harlem) crew, that Nicky Barnes used the addict as a quality tester to determine a batch of heroin's potency.[21] I heard a rumor in the streets that the Smithsonian Museum in Washington, D.C., wanted the hand to archive for educational purposes, but Claw refused to part with it, and died in the early 80s—probably of organ failure—with his hand intact. Frank Lucas, was a drug trafficker turn government informant who operated in Harlem during the late 1960s and early 1970s. He was known for cutting out middlemen and buying heroin directly from his source in Southeast Asia. Lucas boasted that he smuggled heroin in the coffins of dead American servicemen. Lucas had such a colorful life that a film was made about him: in 2007, *American Gangster* starring Denzel Washington hit movie theaters.[22]

On June 5, 1977, the Sunday cover of the *New York Times Maga-zine* in section 6 read: "'Mister Untouchable' This is Nicky Barnes. The Police Say He May Be Harlem's Biggest Drug Dealer. But Can They Prove It?" Leroy Nicholas "Nicky" Barnes was on

---

[21] Flicker, Jonah. "Mr. Untouchable." LAS Magazine, 30 October 2007, http://lostatsea.net/feature.phtml?-fid=8008673454727dce1204db

[22] Alfred W. McCoy, Cathleen B. Reach, and Leonard D. Adams, The Politics of Heroin in Southeast Asia, Harper & Row, 1972.

the cover, his pose arrogant. He was clean shaven and dapper, wearing designer glasses and a custom-made denim suit with a baby-blue shirt and the pièce de résistance, a tie in patriotic red, white, and blue. It was this act of defiance that would one day offend President Jimmy Carter and lead to Barnes' downfall.[23]

Barnes became one of the most infamous drug dealers in New York during the 1970s. In 1972, Barnes formed The Council, a seven-man African American organized crime syndicate that controlled a significant part of the heroin trade in Harlem. Barnes led The Council into an international trafficking ring, which they ran in partnership with the Italian American Mafia until Barnes' arrest in 1978. Barnes was sentenced to life imprisonment, eventually becoming a federal informant that led to the collapse of The Council in 1983.

Although Frank Lucas and Nicky Barnes may have been some of the biggest heroin dealers in Harlem, there have been many books— including *Dark Alliance*, *The Politics of Heroin in Southeast Asia*, *Cocaine Politics*—and investigations by journalists Gary Webb, Alexander Cockburn, and Larry Collins that detail how the United States Central Intelligence Agency (CIA) was actually the drug game's top players, the direct connect who could get drugs into the United States without arousing suspicion.

The government would have us believe Lucas and Barnes were the main source of the drug problem, the most critical factor in flooding Harlem with heroin. But nothing could be further from the truth.

This was the Harlem that Fritz and his siblings found themselves in. The history that shaped Harlem would also shape the futures of Richard Allen Simmons aka Fritz and his family.

---

23   Roberts, Sam. "Nicky Barnes, 'Mr. Untouchable' of Heroin Dealers, Is Dead at 78." The New York Times, 8 June 2019, https://www.nytimes.com/2019/06/08/nyregion/nicky-barnes-dead.html

"To me, the thing that is worse than death is betrayal. You see, I could conceive death, but I could not conceive betrayal."

—Malcolm X

1960s

CHAPTER ONE

Who That Knocking On My Door?

It was a calm, cool day in rural, segregated Charleston, South Carolina on October 8, 1957. Forty-year-old Mae was in labor in her dimly lit bedroom. Her hair was wet with sweat, her face red from the strain of pushing. She took a deep breath and screamed in pain from another contraction. Sweat dripped down her face as Mae's ten-year-old daughter, Evelyn, wiped her brow with a wet cloth. The midwife, a big woman, sat on old wooden stool at Mae's feet.

"I can see the head, Mae. Just a few more pushes."

Mae took another deep breath and pushed with all she had. "That's it. Keep goin', Mae. This'll be the last push."

Mae pushed again. "That's it!"

The crown of the baby's head showed. Mae pushed and pushed.

The midwife eased the head and shoulders out, then the rest of the baby cleared the birth canal. The baby cried out. The midwife put the child on Mae's chest and cut the umbilical cord.

"It's a boy!" Evelyn shouted and kissed the baby's forehead. "What we gonna call him, Momma?"

"Richard Allen Simmons."

Richard was dark as night, beautiful, with a head full of curly hair. He was born at the end of the 50s, in a racially segregated south. The Jim Crow laws mandated racial segregation in all public facilities in the former Confederate States of America (i.e. slave-holding states—South Carolina, North Carolina, Mississippi, Florida, Alabama, Georgia, Louisiana, Texas, Arkansas, Tennessee, and Virginia). The states that were not officially part of the Union or the Confederacy, the Border States (which included Maryland, West Virginia, Delaware, Kentucky, and Missouri) all engaged in legalized slavery as well.[24]

Black southerners were getting restless and civil rights protests were on the rise. They were tired of the lynchings: In 1955 14-year-old Emmett Louis Till was killed in Mississippi, after being accused of offending a white woman. White men took him away, beat him, and mutilated him before shooting him in the head and sinking his body in the Tallahatchie River.[25] They were also tired of whites believing black children weren't smart enough to be taught alongside whites. In 1954, Linda Brown became the poster girl for education equality in the landmark U.S. Supreme Court case, Brown v. Board of Education of Topeka, which ruled school segregation illegal.[26]

---

[24] History.com Editors. "Jim Crow Laws." History, A&E Television Networks, 28 February 2018, https://www.history.com/ topics/early-20th-century-us/jim-crow-laws.

[25] Biography.com Editors. "Emmett Till Biography." The Biography.com, 2 April 2014, https://www.biography.com/ crime-figure/emmett-till.

[26] History.com Editors. "Brown v. Board of Education." History, A&E Television Networks, 27 October 2009, https://www. history.com/ topics/black-history/brown-v-board-of-education-of-topeka.

While Mae was living 760 miles away in the segregated south raising her children, Richard's father, Clifford Harrison, was living up north in New York, the first city in the world to have a black population of over one million. Clifford lived in Harlem, known as "the capital of black America." He was near 7th Avenue and 125th Street, the heart of Harlem known as the Black Times Square. Clifford was often called the Nat King Cole of Harlem. He was a handsome man, wore tailor made suits and a Marcel Wave hairstyle. His skin was smooth and dark against his pearly white teeth and broad smile that lit up a room and made women notice him.

Clifford was living in West Central Harlem with his in-laws, Elizabeth (a housekeeper at New York Hospital, now called New York-Presbyterian/Weill Cornell Medical Center) and Claude Robinson (a veteran, retired city worker, and member of DC 37, New York City's largest public employee union). Clifford's wife, Wilhelmina, pregnant with his son, Junior, and his daughter, Sheila, lived with them.

Clifford wanted more for his family. He was determined to move his wife and children out of their crowded living arrangement. He worked 9 to 5 at John F. Kennedy Airport. He was a part of the ground crew, handling baggage and cleaning planes. He often worked overtime and took odd jobs for the extra cash—even if some of the jobs were illegal, as long as the risks were minimal.

Seventeen-year-old Evelyn and six-year-old Richard visited their father in Harlem, as it was Clifford's way of bonding with his family. It was their third visit and Sheila and Junior were happy—they loved when their siblings came up north. Sheila was excited, knowing she and Evelyn would have a great time playing with her dolls. Evelyn wasn't a city girl. She didn't like to run the streets; Charleston was more her speed. Being the oldest, she was the conservative one and a second mom to her younger siblings. Sheila confided in Evelyn about a lot of things, and she never once made Sheila feel like she didn't want her around. There were times Sheila would sit on the bed and watch her try on several different outfits just to go to the store. It was a major production. Evelyn spent a lot of time in the mirror combing her hair, making sure every strand was in place. Elizabeth would ask, "Who you think you are going to meet at the store?"

"Nobody. A lady should always take pride in how she looks," Evelyn would say.

Junior bored easily, had a hard time keeping still or focused on one thing, and had few friends. Richard was the only person Junior listen too, because of the quality time they spent together when Richard came to town. Junior also knew it would be a great time to show off his GI Joe action figures and race car set with his brother Richard. They were a perfect family when they all came together, Clifford made sure of that.

Sometime in the wee hours of the morning on Tuesday, April 9th, 1963 Clifford's brother, Billie, came knocking on the Robinsons' door. The lights were out, the streets were quiet except for the patter of rain, and everyone was asleep.

The knocking soon turned into pounding that finally woke Elizabeth and Claude.

"Who that knocking on my door?" Elizabeth shouted. She was a petite, feisty woman in her fifties, no nonsense and protective of her family.

Elizabeth fussed as she got out of bed and Claude went back to sleep. Sheila heard the stomping of her feet across the parquet floor. She was curious to see who was knocking. Sheila quietly slipped out of bed and tiptoed to the bedroom door so as not to wake Evelyn, who slept in the bed across from her. Richard and Junior, who shared a room down the hall, stayed sound asleep.

Sheila peeked out and saw Elizabeth with her eyes half open, a scarf tied around her head and leather slippers on her tiny feet, hurrying to the door.

Clifford's brother Billie was a cop in the NYPD. He was a short stocky man with curly hair and a face hard like stone, which he probably developed from all the years on the police force, working in high-crime, drug-infested neighborhoods. His clothes were soaked from the rain. Sheila was surprised to see Billie dressed in his police uniform. *Shouldn't he be out looking for criminals to arrest?* she thought. Instead, Billie was standing at her door in the dead of night, wet from head to toe.

"Sorry to wake you, Mrs. Robinson, but I need to speak with my brother," Billie said in his usual stern tone. "Clifford got in late from work and just went to sleep," Elizabeth said.

"It's real important," Billie assured her.

"What could be so important at this hour, boy?" Elizabeth asked. "I just—I need to speak with my brother please..." Billie said.

Elizabeth relented and hurried to get her husband. On her way to Wilhelmina and Clifford's bedroom, Elizabeth noticed Sheila was up.

"Girl, get your butt back in bed—it's late," Elizabeth scolded. Sheila ran and jumped back in bed, covering her head with the sheets. Elizabeth woke up Clifford and he and Billie sat in the living room talking. Their voices were low so no one could hear. Soon after,

Billie left and Clifford got dressed.

Sheila could tell the lights were on in her parents' bedroom. She figured her father was heading back to work. There were times when he had to go in because someone didn't show up. Since he had a family to take care of, he didn't mind putting in the extra hours.

When Sheila was sure her grandmother was back in bed, she got up and hurried down the hall to catch Clifford before he left to give him a kiss goodnight. The last thing he said to

Sheila was, "Daddy will see you later. Be a good girl for Grandma and Grandpa."

The next day, sometime in the morning around 11:45AM, they got a knock at the door. It was two police officers letting them know that Clifford was dead.

The children often asked their grandparents what happened to Clifford after he died. The question was always avoided to protect them from the truth. Not knowing the particulars behind Clifford's death, with their mother shut off in her bedroom most of the day, made them more curious. A few months after Clifford's death, Sheila was in the kitchen helping Elizabeth prepare dinner and finally gathered enough courage to ask again what happened.

Elizabeth told Sheila her father had held up a bar with some friends and he was shot by the police. Sheila found this hard to accept and believe. *Daddy, a thief? But he had a job at the airport.* The news was difficult to hear. *This can't be true, but why would Grandma lie to me? She loved me too much to do that.* None of it made any sense to her.

On Tuesday, April 9, 1963, Clifford's robbery made The *New York Times*. The headline read: "Gunman Is Killed In Police Battle."[27] The robbery took place at the Blue Moon Bar on 3964½ White Plains Road and 224th Street. According to the article, five heavily armed men, including Clifford, entered the Bronx tavern at 9:20 AM. They robbed the owner, eight patrons, and a barmaid of money and jewelry. A passerby saw the armed men jump into a getaway car, noted the license plate, and notified the police.

Two patrolmen, Donald Collins and Peter Mador of the 45th Precinct, spotted the car a few blocks away from the bar and asked

---

[27] "Gunman Is Killed In Police Battle" New York Times (1923-Current File); April 9, 1963 ProQuest Historical Newspaper: The New York Times with Index pg.50

them to pull over. The robbers immediately got out of the car and began firing their weapons at the cops.

When it was all over a total of 14 shots were fired. One accomplice was critically wounded and Richard's father, Clifford Harrison, was shot twice in the head by Officer Mador, who later received the NYPD Sergeant's Benevolent Association's Medal of Honor for his actions.[28]

Word on the street was that the robbery was orchestrated by someone close to the family. Word also was, it wasn't Clifford's first heist. According to Elizabeth, there were many red flags that night; Billie's visit was one of them. Her sixth sense was kicking in and she felt something wasn't right. Billie never came to the house that late, but that night he was persistent and wouldn't back down. Elizabeth wondered why he couldn't wait to talk to his brother at a decent hour.

When the police came knocking on the door to notify Elizabeth of the incident, she had been unaware of Clifford's illegal activities. Yes, Clifford was a rolling stone, but he was a good husband and father, according to Sheila. He was a provider, helping Elizabeth and Claude with the rent even though he didn't have to. He was the son they never had. He was kind; he never spoke a harsh word to his wife, Wilhelmina or Richard and his siblings. He was never confrontational. He didn't drink or smoke, not even at social gatherings. Clifford was loyal to a fault, especially to those in his inner circle, and it may have cost him his life.

After Clifford's funeral, his brother Billie stopped coming around, and Wilhelmina and the children saw less and less of that side of the family. No one came by to comfort them; Sheila always wondered why. The gossip and arguing behind closed

---

[28] SunJournal.com Editors. "Peter Mador Sr." Sun Journal, 30 September 2011, https://www.sunjournal.com/2011/09/30/peter-mador-sr/

doors in the family revolved around who was really responsible for Clifford's death.

Clifford and Billie's mother, Mary, washed her hands of the children; she didn't want the responsibility of caring for Richard and his three siblings, although she always had her hand out when Clifford was alive. Clifford's father, Gene, was a kind, good-hearted man. Mary was mean and dominated their relationship. She would always yell at the children when they visited. Elizabeth didn't yell at the children and didn't want anyone else doing it, so they stopped going to Clifford's parents' house.

Mary was ashamed to find out that her son was a thief. But she had never questioned where Clifford got the cash, he gave her when the bank was going to foreclose on their home. As a cop, Billie had the better job, but he never offered a dime. Richard, his sisters, and brother could never be embarrassed by what their dad did. He did what he had to in order to care for his family.

Clifford's death set off a chain reaction that tore the fabric of their family apart. It was the turning point for Wilhelmina, Evelyn, Richard, Sheila, and Junior. And nothing would ever be the same.

CHAPTER TWO

The Boogeyman Is Here

WILHELMINA WAS DEVASTATED BY CLIFFORD'S murder, and it took a long time for the children to accept the fact that he wasn't coming back. Clifford was Wilhelmina's first love. She never knew another man. She was heartbroken and lost without him. Alcohol became her vice, a sedative that helped her ease the pain so she could sleep at night. Then she started sleeping all day. She stopped taking the children to school and helping them with their homework. The hugs and goodnight kisses ended as well. It confused and hurt the children that Wilhelmina no longer communicated with them, that she was just a shell of who she used to be.

Before Clifford died, Wilhelmina was caring and soft-spoken. She wore her long wavy hair up in a pompadour hairstyle. She loved to dress up and always had a smile on her face. But now the light in her eyes was gone. Whenever the children asked Elizabeth what was wrong with Wilhelmina they'd always get the same answer: "Mom is not feeling well today."

The children wondered when their mother would finally start to feel better, and if she was so sick, why wasn't she in the hospital?

At the time, they didn't understand that her sickness wasn't physical but mental.

"Stop bothering your momma," Elizabeth would say to the children. "If you need anything, ask me."

It was hard for the children to see their mother go through what they later recognized as an emotional breakdown. Sheila started to think that looking at them every day reminded her mom too much of Clifford and the good times they'd shared. Without Clifford there'd be no more picnics, cookouts, bus rides, or holiday gatherings. Evelyn and Richard's annual visits from the south would be few, if any at all, now that Clifford was gone. How they missed the drive-in movies Clifford took them to. As a family, they were always on an adventure, and it was always fun, even with all the good-natured bickering. Someone was always complaining about something: put the window up, put the window down, it's too cold, it's too hot. It was funny for the children to watch their father struggle to attach the speaker to the car and adjust the volume to get the sound just right. They did everything together and had a lot of laughs.

Richard's father, Clifford did it all for his family. They missed him terribly; missed his face, his laugh, and the good times they shared. But as the months passed, the love and security the children felt when Clifford was alive became a distant memory.

A couple of years after Clifford's death, Wilhelmina started fixing herself up and going out again. Richard and his siblings were happy at first, figuring things were finally getting back to normal, but she began spending more time out and less time with her children.

One day Richard's sister, Sheila was playing on the stoop when Wilhelmina came out smelling really good, with her hair done and wearing a fancy dress.

"Hey, baby," Wilhelmina said, kissing Sheila then hurrying off. Sheila wanted to know where she was going, so she followed her around the corner to 133rd Street and 8th Avenue and watched her mother approach a man Sheila had never seen before—and kiss him.

The man Wilhelmina was kissing was dark, darker than Clifford and Richard. His skin was a deep, charcoal black. *What's Mom doing with him?* Sheila wondered. When they started to walk off, Sheila ran up to her. "Where you going?" Sheila asked, with some attitude.

Wilhelmina looked down at Sheila with her eyebrows arched and her mouth twisted to the side. "Sheila, you're not supposed to be around the corner," she said sternly.

Sheila was the bold and sassy one of her siblings. She was an inquisitive child, and there was no stopping her when she wanted to know something—which Wilhelmina knew about her.

Sheila didn't care if her mother was mad. Wilhelmina was right around the corner, so why couldn't Sheila follow? Even though Clifford had been gone for a few years, Sheila still felt betrayed when she saw her mother kiss that man. It made it even more final that Clifford was never coming back.

"Well, who is that?" Sheila pressed on.

"This is LeRoy," Wilhelmina said. She gestured to him. "LeRoy, this is my daughter, Sheila."

LeRoy raised his eyebrows and several wrinkles appeared on his forehead. The awkward expression on his face and a half-ass smile revealed that Wilhelmina hadn't mentioned having children. Then and there, Sheila decided she didn't like LeRoy. Feeling like they were some secret hidden away from him made Sheila dislike him even more.

Sheila would later learn LeRoy Walker was a veteran who lived with his Uncle Mack and Aunt Alice Walker on West 133rd Street.

Sheila looked him up and down, rolled her eyes, and poked out her lips. "Um." What she wanted to say was, *Why you talking to that nigga? You ain't been with anybody since Daddy died and you don't need anybody. We can make you happy. What the fuck you need from him?* Sheila was itching to tell her mother this, but knew better than to say a word out loud.

"Am I gonna see you later?" Sheila asked instead. "Yeah," her mother said.

As Sheila was about to go back home a second man crossed the street. He also greeted Wilhelmina like they knew each other.

"Mr. Mack, this is my daughter, Sheila," Wilhelmina said.

He bent down with his big round face, pudgy nose, and wide lips to Sheila's level and gave her a warm, friendly smile. "Hey, precious, how you doing?"

"Fine."

"What's going on?" Mr. Mack asked. "Nothing," Sheila said, frowning. "You a beautiful little thing." "Thank you."

"Make sure you come around and see Uncle Mack some time."

How the fuck you my Uncle Mack? Don't you have to be in my family?

Sheila thought. She was confused. She knew Mr. Mack could tell by the way her nose scrunched up and her eyebrows knitted tightly together on her brow. Sheila couldn't wait to tell Junior, Richard, and Evelyn everything she had seen and heard.

Richard and Junior were playing at the P.S. 92 schoolyard. Sheila hurried over, pulled Richard aside and told him about the entire encounter, including Uncle Mack. Sheila wanted Richard to explain to her how they had family nearby that they didn't know.

"We don't have no got damn Uncle Mack," Richard said.

He didn't believe Sheila. He was hungry, so they walked to the corner candy store for some snacks. While they were at the register Uncle Mack walked in.

"There he goes right there," Sheila shouted, pointing at him.

"He who?" Richard asked and turned around. "We don't know that damn man, Sheila."

"Uncle Mack, Uncle Mack," Sheila called out. "This is my brother right here. You know him?"

Uncle Mack looked at Sheila with an amused smile on his face. "No, baby," he said, shaking his head. He smiled and explained that because Wilhelmina was seeing his nephew, LeRoy, it made him an honorary uncle.

"Your mom seeing *who*?" Richard asked and turned to Sheila. "What the fuck he mean?"

Sheila's mouth fell open. Cursing around elders was a no-no. Sheila could tell it had slipped out.

Uncle Mack pretended not to hear him. "Y'all take care," he said, and quickly left the store.

"Your mom ain't seeing nobody," Richard said as they walked outside. He didn't want to believe it.

"Yes, she is. She's seeing his nephew, fool," Sheila insisted.

"Your momma ain't seeing nobody," Richard repeated. He still felt the deep pain of Clifford's death and, like Sheila, resented the idea of another man entering their lives.

"Let's go down the block then," Sheila said. She had to prove she was telling the truth

"We're not supposed to go that far," Richard said. "I know… but who gonna know but us two?"

Richard got an eyeful the minute they turned onto 133rd Street.

LeRoy sat on the stoop with Wilhelmina on his lap. Richard was speechless. His eyes locked on the couple.

"We got ta go," Sheila said, suddenly worried that Richard might physically confront LeRoy. She pulled him back down the street before any neighbors recognized them.

When they got back to P.S. 92, Junior, a small frame guy, with a barely combed afro was arguing with another black boy. Junior and the boy had made a bet over a pitch-and-toss game. Apparently Junior had won but the other boy wouldn't pay up.

Junior was stub-born, a risk taker who lacked patience, was fearless, and never backdown from a fight.

"How much the guy owes you?" Richard demanded.

"That nigga owes me $100. He bet me that he could toss his quarter farther than mine. He didn't and now I want my money," Junior said

"Let it be, that nigga ain't got no $100," Richard responded.

An old man who knew their grandparents walked by and heard Junior yelling. "I'm going to tell your grandfather you out here gambling."

This angered Junior even more. "Mind your business old man and go head on," Junior yelled back. Junior was the real rebel in the family and had grown withdrawn and disinterested since his father's death.

"You just like getting your ass whooped. Is that a turn-on for you or what?" Richard asked Junior. "I never seen someone who likes getting their ass beat as much as you do."

Richard may as well have been talking to a brick wall.

"He better give me something," Junior said, repeating himself over and over until the boy handed him a ten-dollar bill.

The old man who yelled at Junior lived nearby and knew their grandparents, Elizabeth and Claude, just like everyone else in the neighborhood did. They were also part of a community social club, so it was only a matter of time before they heard about the confrontation. Sure enough, when Richard and Sheila got home the old man was standing in the Robinsons' living room. Claude was usually easygoing with the children and left the disciplining to his wife. If Claude thought or heard that his grandchildren disrespected an elder, however, there was no holding back his wrath. He was old school and believed in old-school respect, that children should be seen and not heard, and no matter what, always respect your elders.

Claude didn't even greet the children. All he wanted to know was, were Sheila and Richard there? They looked at each other and shrugged, playing dumb. They were very protective of one another after Clifford passed and didn't want to see Junior get in trouble.

"They were standing right there," the old man said.

Sheila and Richard finally admitted they were there but denied hearing Junior disrespect the old man. Junior didn't get a beating for that particular incident, but Claude definitely reprimanded him. Junior had an attitude, and the family knew that if he didn't straighten up, it would be a problem later on. Richard told Junior, "That attitude may work for you, but not for us." Richard and Sheila knew they had to keep an eye on their younger brother. If they didn't, Junior's hard head and temper would someday get him into real trouble. The siblings had deep love for each other. They may have had different mothers, but they never considered using the word "half." They were simply brothers and sisters, and they always had one another's back.

Richard was a diplomat, a thinker, an organizer who led by example and believed in respecting others. Unlike Junior, he was also low-key, knowing how to sit back and observe, or feel out a situation.

Although he was laidback and wanted things to be easy, Richard was no angel. His idea of fun always took things to an extreme. The kids had a food fight ritual, which involved using water and whatever food was nearby. It started because Richard was bored and needed a good laugh. He knew the best attack was the least expected one.

Richard and Evelyn were up north for the summer and staying with Elizabeth and Claude. One hot day, Richard and Sheila were alone in the house. Junior was outside somewhere, and Evelyn had gone to the store. Sheila was washing dishes when she felt something hard on her back. Richard had hit her with a raw egg. She could feel the cold, slimy yolk and pieces of cracked shell sliding down her back soaking through her tank top, and down inside the waistband of her Gloria Vanderbilt jeans.

"Okay," Sheila said, nodding, a sinister grin on her face. She immediately plotted revenge.

Sheila finished the dishes and changed her shirt. At this point Richard was in the shower—it was the perfect opportunity for payback. She filled a pot with ice-cold water, climbed up on the toilet seat, pulled the curtain back, and threw it on him. She'd never laughed so hard, and hearing Richard scream made her laugh even harder as she ran out of the bathroom.

"Oh okay, you going in like that!" Richard shouted. It was a war cry. He got out of the shower, got dressed, and the fight was on.

Whatever Richard and Sheila could get their hands on they threw at each other, running and ducking to avoid flying objects. They were having a good time and not watching the clock. Then Richard grabbed a bag of flour out of the kitchen cabinet and threw it all over Sheila. She had just gone to the beauty parlor earlier that day and was now covered from head to toe in flour. She no longer found Richard's game funny and was pissed. She grabbed a bottle of dishwashing liquid and squeezed, squirting it all over him and the floor as he ran away. The payback was giving Sheila an adrenaline rush. She then filled a small pot with water and threw it at Richard. They were laughing and yelling so loudly that they didn't hear a key turn in the door as Elizabeth and Evelyn walked in.

"What the hell is going on here?" Elizabeth asked.

Richard and Sheila stood still, surprised. Evelyn just shook her head.

"I just went down the block. What the fuck y'all do to this house?" Elizabeth asked.

Elizabeth never beat the children, but Richard and Sheila were sure they were gonna get an ass whipping that day. They were surprised at how calm, cool, and collected Elizabeth was. She didn't even raise her voice, not one time.

"I'ma tell you what I'm gonna do. I'ma go back out to the corner store, but I'll be back," Elizabeth said, then left.

Sheila ran to the window and saw Elizabeth leaving and Claude walking down the block toward the building. "Grandpa coming," she shouted.

Richard and Sheila knew they had to clean up fast, because Claude was the one that would bust your ass. Evelyn refused to help them and disappeared into a bedroom. Richard and Sheila ran around that apartment like a tornado, cleaning up everything, leaving no evidence behind. The house was spic and span when they were done.

Unfortunately, Sheila was still covered in flour. Claude let himself in, then stopped dead in his tracks when he saw Sheila.

"I need you to explain how you got all that *got damn* flour in your hair and all over your clothes," Claude said, looking at Sheila up and down. He seemed baffled.

"I was playing," Sheila answered.

"Playing how?"

Sheila looked over at Richard a few feet away. Richard was busy looking at the ceiling. Sheila knew he couldn't put together an excuse. She made up a story.

"I was pretending to be the Abominable Snowman."

"You think I'm a fool. You just made that up." When Sheila tried to defend herself, he said, "Sheila, you are not a good liar."

Elizabeth had already told Claude what they'd done. He just wanted to hear what Sheila was going to say.

"I'm not gonna beat your ass this time, but don't ever let me hear y'all were in here playing with food again." Claude then slipped his hand into his pocket and pulled out some money. "Now go back to that *got damn* beauty parlor and ask Ms. Dorothy if she can do your hair again."

Deep down, Claude was a softy who would rather reason with the children than whip them. He preferred making threats, hoping they would scare the kids straight.

The seriousness of Wilhelmina and LeRoy's relationship became apparent when she brought him over to meet the family. Claude didn't care for her new boyfriend and didn't want LeRoy in his house ever again. Claude was easy-going, but never bit his tongue when it came to things or people he disapproved of. He couldn't put his finger on it right away, but there was something about LeRoy he didn't like. A month later, Wilhelmina packed her things, left Sheila and Junior behind with Elizabeth and Claude, and moved around the corner with LeRoy and Mr. and Mrs. Mack Walker.

ELIZABETH AND CLAUDE SENT SHEILA and Junior to the Fresh Air Fund camp for two weeks that summer. Richard and Evelyn couldn't make it because their mother, Mae became ill, and wanted her children close to home.

Sheila and Junior came back from camp and couldn't wait to see their mom. They dumped their stuff and hurried to the Walkers' house to visit. They were so happy to see her. They sat around talking for a while, catching her up on their vacation.

When LeRoy walked in the house he didn't say anything to the children or act like he even saw them. He just started cursing and calling Wilhelmina all kinds of names. Sheila held Junior's hand tight and sat still on the couch. Suddenly LeRoy pulled his hand back as if he were holding a tennis racket and slapped Wilhelmina, leaving large red fingerprints on the side of her face. Junior and Sheila had never seen their mother get hit or cursed out by anyone—certainly not by their father, Clifford. They didn't know how to react; they were more in shock than frightened. Finally Uncle Mack heard the commotion and came rushing in from a back room.

"Boy you crazy, hitting on this woman? That girl got a father who knows a lot of people. I don't want no problems," Uncle Mack said.

"Mom, let's go," Sheila said.

"I'm all right, I'm all right," Wilhelmina insisted. "Let's go," Junior said to Sheila, standing up.

They left quickly, running home to tell their grandmother, Elizabeth.

"I don't want y'all going around there anymore," Elizabeth said. "Mr. Mack is nice, but I don't want y'all in that house."

Sheila and Junior never went back. LeRoy and Wilhelmina left Uncle Mack's house shortly after, moving to the Highbridge section of the Bronx. Once they settled into their new home, Wilhelmina came to her parents' house, packed her children's things, and took Junior and Sheila to the Bronx. If they'd had a choice, Sheila and Junior would have stayed with their grandparents. But they were never given one.

The summer was almost over. Sheila and Junior felt Richard and Evelyn's absence. It was a weird, eerie feeling like something was missing and the happier times seemed to be fading away. Sheila and Junior spoke with them often on the phone, but at some point it became clear Richard and Evelyn weren't coming back anytime soon. The calls were few and far in between. Sheila and Junior didn't see Richard and Evelyn for the next five years.

CHAPTER THREE

The Boogeyman's Reign Of Fear

WILHELMINA MARRIED LeRoy AFTER SHE moved Sheila and Junior to the Bronx. A couple of months after the marriage, they had a son, TyRay. Sheila didn't like that Junior and her, at ages six and seven, had to share a bedroom. The bathroom became Sheila's dressing room. Within weeks of the move, their stepfather's home became their prison and LeRoy the warden. They spoke less and less to their grandparents and their siblings, Richard and Evelyn were in South Carolina. When LeRoy went to work, he put a lock on the rotary telephone in the bedroom and took the touch-tone cords from the kitchen phone. LeRoy monitored all of their phone calls and limited their visits to their grandpa-rents' house. Within the space of a couple of weeks Sheila and Junior went from being happy children to living in fear.

Not having access to a phone almost cost TyRay his life. One day he wasn't feeling well and had a slight fever. Hours later the fever got dangerously high and they needed an ambulance quick.

It was late and LeRoy still wasn't home, so the rotary phone was locked and the cords to the kitchen phone gone. Wilhelmina grabbed a hammer from the utility drawer and hit the lock, breaking it as well as the rotary phone.

Wilhelmina was frantic. "Quick, run to the neighbor's house and get help now!" she yelled.

Sheila saw the panic in her mother's eyes and heard the urgency in her voice. Sheila ran to the next-door neighbor's house and called Elizabeth for help. Elizabeth gave Sheila an old home remedy over the phone: give the baby a lukewarm bath, chop onions and put them into two handkerchiefs, then tie one around each wrist. Somehow it worked and TyRay's fever broke.

After that, Sheila was determined to find a way to access the house phone. She couldn't get a copy of the key to the lock but found a variety store in the neighborhood and bought phone cords for the kitchen phone. Sheila would sneak calls to Richard and Evelyn down south when LeRoy was out, then stuff the cords in a shoe inside a shoebox that she hid in her bedroom closet.

Sheila always believed there was an angel watching over TyRay, even before he was born. When Wilhelmina was pregnant with him, she and LeRoy had a disagreement while he was drunk. Sheila didn't know why they were arguing—they were always fighting about something. That night the argument went too far. Suddenly, Wilhelmina called out to Sheila from the living room. Sheila found her bent over, moaning in pain, and holding her belly. Blood was everywhere and LeRoy was nowhere to be found.

"Call an ambulance," Wilhelmina said.

The ambulance and police arrived. EMS evaluated Wilhelmina's injuries at the apartment. Wilhelmina had a knife wound on the left side of her stomach that required stitches. As she was being carried away on a stretcher, a cop interrogated her. She covered up for LeRoy, who'd almost killed their unborn child. She told the officers she slipped on some water while putting away the dishes and fell onto the knife. The officers knew the signs of domestic violence, but could not force Wilhelmina to press charges. Sheila and Junior stayed with Elizabeth until their mother was released from the hospital.

Wilhelmina didn't put much effort into caring for TyRay after he was born—that was Sheila's job. She had him, but Sheila raised him. At seven, Sheila didn't know what it meant to be a child anymore, because she was too busy parenting Junior and TyRay. Wilhelmina drank and slept most the day. Often she couldn't get up in the mornings because of the beatings she'd received from LeRoy the night before.

Sheila had to nurse both her mother and the new baby. Sheila bathed and put TyRay to bed at night and laid out his clothes and hers for the next day. Sheila prepared his bottles, fed him in the morning, and came home for lunch to feed him again. TyRay was a good baby, but like most he fussed and cried. In his terrible twos, he required a lot of patience. There was also the pressure of calming TyRay down before LeRoy got home. LeRoy worked long hours and didn't want to come home to a toddler's nonstop crying.

"You better shut that little muthafucker up," LeRoy would say.

TyRay was at his mothers's feet, grabbing her legs and reaching for her to pick him up. On this particular day, she was weak and not feeling well, so Sheila picked TyRay up off the floor, put him on her hip, and bounced him up and down.

"Hush, TyRay. Hush," Sheila said.

But Sheila couldn't stop him from crying. He twisted and turned in her arms, wailing for Wilhelmina. When Sheila put him down, he started crawling toward her. That's when LeRoy walked over, still wearing his work boots, and kicked TyRay so hard he flew down the hallway. TyRay lay still, his crying finally stopped.

Junior, who was standing in the doorway of their bedroom, saw everything. There was a look of terror on his face.

Sheila thought TyRay was dead. *You going to jail now,* she thought.

Sheila ran down the hallway and checked to see if he was still breathing. She picked him up. TyRay had urinated and defecated on himself. His little face was swollen and his nose bloody. She took him to the bathroom to wash him and wipe the blood off his face. Even at the innocent age of two, the pain he was in was so obvious to Sheila. He rested his head on Sheila's shoulder, moaning and whimpering softly. "It's going to be okay," Sheila said to him as she rubbed his back.

Wilhelmina never took TyRay to the hospital. He slept with Sheila that night. Sheila always kept him close after that.

LeRoy was a college graduate and war veteran who worked for the New York City Department of Sanitation. He was strict and ran the house with an iron fist. Sheila knew how to manage a household by the time she was nine years old.

Sheila was always cleaning, whether it was washing the dishes or wiping down the stove, turning bed mattresses, doing the laundry, keeping the mirrors free of smudges and fingerprints, scrubbing the bathroom clean on her knees with a pail and sponge, washing floors and walls, flipping and fluffing sofa cushions, and polishing and dusting furniture. It was relentless and an overwhelming amount of work and responsibility for a young girl. LeRoy walked around the house and double-checked everything Sheila and Junior did. He whipped Sheila one day with an extension cord for not drying out the sink after washing the dishes. Everything had painful consequences if it wasn't done right or to his liking. Sheila despised all the cleaning. She felt punished every day.

LeRoy complained about Junior's cleaning and whipped him too. One night, LeRoy came home late and found that Junior had forgotten to take the garbage out. While Junior was sleeping, he came into the bedroom with the kitchen wastebasket in one hand and a belt in the other. He beat Junior, waking him up, then dumped the trash—the empty cans and bottles, the soiled food containers and plastic wrappings of raw meat, everything—on top of Junior.

"You'll take the fuckin' shit out next time, won't you!" LeRoy said as he beat Junior across the back with the belt.

LeRoy then made Junior pick up the trash and take it outside. The stench in the room was strong and made Sheila want to gag. Sheila started to help Junior by sweeping up the trash that was left behind and changing his bedsheets.

Afterward, Junior took a shower, but LeRoy wasn't finished disciplining him. As soon as Junior turned off the water, LeRoy beat him again. The second beating was much worse because his body was still wet. The welts looked like he had been beaten with a horse whip, leaving parts of his body red and raw. Sheila didn't like seeing her brother get beat. She couldn't take the hollering, the sound the belt made when it made contact with his skin. Sheila would cover her ears to block it all out. She always resented LeRoy for those beatings.

The household was run like a military training camp and LeRoy was the drill sergeant. There was no such thing as sleeping in on Saturdays.

"Time to get up, let's go," LeRoy would shout at five in the morning.

Without hesitation, Junior and Sheila immediately hopped out of bed, making their sheets neat. The fold had to be tight enough that LeRoy could bounce a coin off it. After tidying their rooms, they brushed their teeth, washed their faces, and got dressed. They would then meet LeRoy in the living room, and he'd divide the chores and tedious tasks like polishing all their shoes, wiping down their sneakers, and washing the shoestrings. Sheila had to wash all the clothes, starch, iron, mend tears, and sew on missing buttons. She had to fold socks military style, placing two socks on top of the other, rolling them up tightly starting at the toe, and then open the outside sock and pull it back around. Sheila used the military roll for clothes, too. Everything going in their drawers needed to be rolled very tightly for space, and to prevent wrinkles. If one thing was out of place, LeRoy would dump everything out and make them start all over. He would also sometimes wake up the children in the middle of the night to clean their room.

Every hanger had to be lined the same way. The shirts, pants, dresses, and skirts each had to have its own section. Shoes had to be lined up neatly. One time, Sheila made the mistake of hanging several garments in the wrong section. LeRoy pulled everything out of the closet, throwing clothes everywhere. Sharp wire hangers flew at Sheila, leaving welts on her arms and legs. Sheila and Junior's lives were like a scene out of *Mommie Dearest*.[29]

Living with LeRoy was like living with Dr. Jekyll and Mr. Hyde. The simplest things would transform him into someone they did not recognize, someone who was evil and frightening. The longer they stayed in that house with LeRoy, the worse things got. The mental and physical abuse he inflicted on Wilhelmina, Richard's siblings, Sheila and Junior was endless.

A few months after Sheila and Junior moved in with Wilhelmina and LeRoy, Junior got a job at the A&P a few blocks away from the house. Junior worked really hard so he could have a few dollars in his pocket, but LeRoy would take it away from

---

[29] Mommie Dearest. Directed by Frank Perry, Paramount Pictures, 1981. Film.

him. LeRoy was a cruel man. Out of the three of Wilhelmina's children, Junior received the most vicious beatings.

LeRoy was an educated man, so going to school, studying hard, and getting good grades was a priority. When report card time rolled around, he would warn Junior and Sheila that they'd better have excellent grades. Sheila loved school and always excelled in her classes.

Junior, on the other hand, never liked school and his report cards usually had plenty of red marks, which always led to more beatings.

LeRoy always tried to keep Sheila and Junior sharp and on their toes. He often challenged them with pop-up questions about math, spelling, and history. They also had to be able to recite the multiplication table without hesitation and know how to read an analog clock.

One day Junior and Sheila were sitting at the dining room table doing their homework when LeRoy came in. Two weeks earlier he'd drawn pictures of analog clocks, with hands that showed different hours and minutes. He expected them to know how to read and write the time on each clock. Sheila was a fast learner, reciting the times quickly. She tried her best to teach Junior, but certain things just didn't come as easily for him.

"What time does that say, Junior?" LeRoy asked, pointing to the paper.

Junior looked to Sheila. She could tell by the expression on his face he didn't know how to read the time. LeRoy had his back to her. She stood off to the side and tried to mouth the answer to him, but Junior couldn't read her lips fast enough.

"Why you looking at Sheila?" LeRoy turned his head toward her. "And you better not say a damn thing," he said to her.

LeRoy then turned back to Junior and saw him looking at the floor. He asked him again to read the time. When LeRoy grew tired of waiting, he picked up a book off the table and hit Junior in the head with a savage blow, knocking him to the floor. Sheila felt useless—she wanted badly to help her brother. She had always tried to do right by Junior, telling him to go to school and to study hard. They tried to be good little children, they truly did, but there was no pleasing LeRoy. Day in and day out, LeRoy beat Junior, breaking him down bit by bit, until there was nothing left but hatred

Junior often talked about running away or killing LeRoy because he didn't want to live this way anymore. One day they came home to find Wilhelmina beaten unconscious. The look on Junior's face that evening scared Sheila.

"Sheila today is the day I'm going to kill him," Junior said. "I don't want you to go to jail," Sheila pleaded.

From that day forward, whenever Junior and Sheila were alone, he'd plot how he was going to kill LeRoy. Sheila knew if he tried something, their mother would not protect them. She loved LeRoy more than her children, that was clear. Sheila and Junior waited to hear her say she'd had enough, but they never heard the words. They wondered if she had a breaking point. If she did, it never came. The children would have told someone but feared they would not have been believed. They didn't even tell their grandparents.

Sheila was more likely to share the truth with her sister, Evelyn, but when she called down south, the number had changed. She'd heard rumors through the family that Richard and Evelyn had left the south and moved to St. Nicholas Projects right in Harlem. Besides that, Sheila didn't have any information for their siblings. Sheila thought all was lost, and that this was her life forever. Little did she know life would get worse before it got better. She would reunite with Richard and Evelyn in Harlem when drugs in the community were at an all-time high. Its adverse effects would not only ravish Harlem but play a major role in their lives.

1970s

CHAPTER FOUR

Before There Was A Fritz

Evelyn and Richard where two peas in a pod. Richard went wherever Evelyn did, so when Evelyn—got fed up with the lack of jobs and low wages in South Carolina—decided to go north to find work, Richard knew he'd leave with her. Evelyn packed her things, then moved her and Richard to the St. Nicholas Projects in Harlem.

Richard adapted to his new home and surroundings quickly, making new friends, and making a name for himself. Richard was a young man always one step ahead of everyone else. He was always thinking outside of the box. He was never afraid to take chances and always marched to the beat of his own drum. He feared nothing and no one, which may have been due to his wrestling and Kung Fu fights he had with his older brothers. They were not Clifford's sons and lived down south with Richard's biological mother, Mae. There were techniques his brothers used, believing the fighting would toughen Richard up. They didn't want him growing up being a gump; a weak spineless, sissy.

Many people believed young Richard had delusions of

grandeur because he dared to be so different. His methods were unique, he treated all people the same. Whether you were an addict or a politician, no one man was better than another in his book. The country boy from down south liked to dream big. He had big ideas and was determined to reach his goal.

Richard was just a teenager when he started generating capital as an entrepreneur. He partnered with his best friend Rob, whom he'd met when he moved into the St. Nicholas projects, along with his cousin Curtis, and Curtis' best friend Danny, to promote parties throughout the city. Richard loved to dance and could hustle like a ballroom professional. On the dance floor he was elegance in motion. If Richard found out there was a party, he and the trio were there, and Richard danced all night, doing the Hustle, and free-styling.

Richard really liked to party, but he also paid attention to the crowd a good party attracted and the cash it generated. He eventually convinced Curtis, Rob, and Danny to throw their own parties. Richard worked out a deal with the director of Salem Center, behind Salem United Methodist Church in the St. Nicholas Housing Projects where he lived. The trio and the director would split the door profits. Rob was the artist, so he created the party flyer. They made copies, distributing them in the St. Nicholas complex and all over Harlem.

The first party was a huge success. As for the profits… Richard had no intention of evenly splitting the profits with the center director. He told Curtis, who was collecting money at the door, to pocket the entry fee of every other person that walked into the party. They made a few hundred dollars, reinvested it in the next party, and so forth. No one was ever the wiser.

They promoted parties for a year. Things were going well with their party promotions. They heard about a popular local DJ working with a promoter who threw parties in a community center in 3333 Broadway. Richard and his partners decided to check him out. He had no idea what the next few hours would bring.

They always stepped out in style when they partied. They went to A.J. Lesters—an expensive and popular men's clothing store on 125th Street—and got their outfits. They wore double knit pants with the matching knit shirts, British Walker shoes, and heavy sheepskin coats.

It was a cold winter night. The community center party was packed with teenagers. The place was jumping when a bunch of older guys suddenly crashed the party and refused to pay. They were loud and ready to fight the party promoters. A security guard showed up with a .45 handgun and let a shot off in the air. "All right, everybody cut it out!" he yelled. But chaos erupted with the gunshot, and suddenly teens were pushing and shoving one another to get out.

Seeing the gun Richard said, "We outta here. Let's go." Richard picked up a folding chair to shield himself, Curtis, Danny, and Rob from the stampeding crowd who was running in all different directions to get out of harm's way. He was making a pathway toward the front entrance when the security guard saw Richard and assumed, he was part of the crew who'd crashed the party. He grabbed Richard by the collar of his sheepskin with one hand and held the .45 in the other.

"Put the chair down," the guard said.

While he had Richard by the collar, the guard's son in his early twenties emerged from the crowd and, without warning, hit Richard on the head with the butt of a 9-millimeter handgun. He knocked Richard out cold and Curtis reacted immediately, hitting the son with the .38 handgun he'd hidden in his jacket. Danny pulled out his .38 and backed everybody off Richard. They then dragged him out of the center. Richard woke once he felt Harlem's winter chill.

"What happened? Who hit me?" Richard was furious. When they told him, he replied, "Fuck that, we going back in!" He planned on getting payback immediately, and Curtis, Rob, and Danny had been down to go back when Archie, a neighborhood friend exiting the party stopped them. "Y'all gotta go, the cops are coming," Archie warned. "I got a car, I'll take y'all home."

They hurried to his blue 1970 Ford Country Squire station wagon and rode off with a screech. As they talked about the incident, Richard got riled up again.

"Yo fuck that! Let me out." Richard yelled, hitting and kicking the back of Archie's seat.

Archie pulled the car over. Richard then got out and walked back toward the party, about a half a mile away. Curtis, Danny, and Rob wanted the night to end and to get home in one piece, but they couldn't let Richard go back alone. That's not the way their crew worked. So they reluctantly trailed behind him. Richard immediately spotted the security guard's son in front of the community center with several friends.

"Gimme a gun," Richard demanded.

Danny checked the gun safety, then handed Richard his .38. Danny was adamant that he not get more riled up. Instead, Richard charged the group of young men.

"What y'all wanna do? I'll fuck all y'all punk ass niggers up!" Richard yelled.

Richard was enraged; he felt no fear. The other teens backed up to let the guys fight one on one, and Richard tucked Danny's gun in his waist to make sure they stayed out of it. He then dished out an ass whupping on the security guard's son and they eventually headed home up Broadway.

A short time later, several cop cars with sirens blaring surrounded Richard and the trio. The security guard's son was in one of the patrol cars and had pointed them out to the cops. The cops threw them up against the patrol cars and frisked them. They found the gun on Richard and took him to jail.

Richard spent a couple of days on Rikers Island while Evelyn gathered bail money. Each day Richard spent behind bars made him angrier. He blamed his cousin Curtis for his situation—he should've had a heads up that they were bringing guns to the party. He really just wanted someone else to blame.

When Richard was released, he found Curtis and Danny in the house waiting for him. Richard didn't want to talk, didn't want to hear nothing, and didn't care who was around. He walked right up to Curtis and before he could react, let off a barrage of heavy blows to his chest. The force behind the punches caused Curtis to stumble back against the wall but he didn't fight back because he believed Richard was right. Curtis also knew that times were changing, and people weren't fighting one-on-one with their hands anymore. He needed to be ready for whatever.

Richard was generally quiet and mild-mannered, but he had a violent side. If you brought trouble or jeopardized his livelihood, he became a completely different person. No one, not even family, could escape his wrath. Danny witnessed this firsthand when they worked a summer job together at Douglas Jr. High back in 1972.

Danny first met Richard on the Central Park Great Lawn near 79th Street. Richard was at football practice, doing backflips with Kennedy

High School's gymnastic team. Danny didn't know Richard at the time, but noticed him because of his grace and style on the wrestling mat.

Danny would see Richard again the following summer at Douglas Jr. High under more serious circumstances. Two neighborhood bullies affiliated with a local gang had picked a fight with Richard over a table game; one picked up a pool stick to hit him. Richard grabbed the stick from him and beat the teen over the head with several vicious blows, leaving him unconscious on the ground in a pool of blood. Richard was chased down by the teen's friends and jumped. Danny would later tell Curtis about that day and learn that the two were cousins.

Richard's victim wound up in the hospital, and his parents pressed criminal charges. There was a trial and Richard went to court with his sister Evelyn by his side. Numerous witnesses took the stand and testified on Richard's behalf, including Danny and the school's program directors. The judge ruled that Richard had acted in self-defense and dismissed all the charges against him. From that day, Danny and Richard's friendship grew. They did everything together after that and whenever Richard called on Danny, he was always there to help without hesitation or question.

Danny's loyalty was tested on a bitterly cold winter day a couple years later in 1975. Richard asked Danny to come with him and Curtis to the Bronx. Richard had gotten a call that his cousin CeCe's house had been robbed. The thief was presumed to be a young Latino man, the building's superintendent. You'd have to have a death wish to mess with Richard's loved ones. Danny had seen what Richard had done to the teenager with the pool stick; he knew that things would not end well for the superintendent. Angering him was like releasing the Kraken from *Clash of the Titans*.[30] But Danny had his back regardless.

Richard, Curtis, and Danny got their guns and headed to the Bronx. It was a quiet afternoon on a weekday—when children were at school and their parents at work—so Richard wasn't worried about witnesses if things got crazy. They staked out the courtyard from CeCe's apartment window, watching from behind the curtains and waiting patiently for the super to show

---

[30] Clash of the Titans, Directed by Desmond Davis, Metro-Goldwyn-Mayer, 1981. Film.

up. When he did, Richard met him in the hallway, snatched him up at gunpoint, and forced him into CeCe's apartment. Richard tied him to a chair with an electrical cord. He then wrapped the cord around the guy's neck and down to his hands. Every time he tried to move, the cord cut off his oxygen and sliced into his throat, choking him. As he asphyxiated, Richard beat him in the face with his .38 until he drew blood.

When Richard was done, the super's lips and face were swollen and his eyes partially shut. Richard untied him and made him strip naked. He forced him into a bath of ice-cold water, then made him stand in front of an open window. It was freezing cold. The super stood dripping wet and shivering. He was terrified as he prayed in Spanish. After a while he stopped praying, because his teeth started chattering until his jaws had locked shut. Richard only stopped when he agreed to return the stolen items.

"If I find out you told anyone about what happened here today, we are coming back," Richard threatened, then made the super get dressed and escort them safely out the building. The super, shaken and battered, stood silently in the doorway until the trio jumped into a car and sped way.

CHAPTER FIVE

The Queen Of The Dunbar

Dunbar Castle was one of the strongest fortresses in Scotland. Circa 1070

IN ANOTHER LIFE QUEEN BEE was a nurse named Joan Moreland. She worked at Sydenham Hospital and her father ran a popular skin hole, or gambling den, in Harlem. Gamblers played the card game George Skin, a favorite among workers from the South. Queen Bee enjoyed hanging out in the skin hole, dating big-time gamblers, and socializing with shady characters and criminals. In the late 1960s Queen Bee left her nurse's uniform behind for good and connected with Vincent C. Papa, Sr., an associate of the Lucchese crime family in New York.

The Corsican Gang, part of the French Mob and headed by Paul Carbone, supplied the United States with 80 to 90 percent of its heroin and the Lucchese Mafia was the distributer. The Corsicans smuggled heroin from Turkey to France and then to the United States through Canada. The operation reached its peak in the late 1960s and early 1970s and was responsible for providing the vast majority of the heroin used in the United States.[31]

Queen Bee was the Luccheses' direct connection to the Harlem addict population. The Lucchese family provided her with kilos of heroin that she distributed throughout Harlem to workers and other dealers. Queen Bee was the first black woman on the East or West Coast to deal exclusively in kilos, which very few people had access to, and rare, for a woman doing business on that level with the mafia. She would become one of Harlem's largest heroin dealers and was known throughout the country as the Queen Bee of the dope game. She was on the same level as Nicky Barnes and Frank Lucas—some say even bigger, at the time. The money Queen Bee made distributing kilos of heroin for Vincent Papa, Sr., afforded her family a lavish lifestyle.

No one thought anyone could stop the Queen's hustle. It would take the Bureau of Narcotics and Dangerous Drugs division, known today as the Drug Enforcement Agency (DEA), to bring her to justice.[32]

Carmine "Mr. Gribbs" Tramunti was born and raised in Harlem. He ran the Harlem Game, one of the major floating craps games in New York. In 1967, following the death of Lucchese boss Tommy Lucchese, Carmine became the official boss of the family.

In 1973, Carmine and other mobsters were indicted on drug charges after law enforcement cracked a major heroin route coming in from France through Canada. The trial was dubbed "The French Connection" and received national headlines.

---

[31] Wikipedia contributors, "French Connection," Wikipedia, The Free Encyclopedia, https://en.wikipedia.org/w/index. php?title=French_Connection&oldid=928508704 (accessed December 2, 2019).

[32] (32a) Jones, Thom L. "The Man Who Stole The French Connection." Gangsters Inc., 2 May 2011, http://gangstersinc. ning.com/profiles/blogs/the-man-who-stole-the-french

Ultimately Carmine was convicted of financing the heroin smuggling operation.[33] Indicted along with Carmine was Papa, Sr.'s longtime partner, Anthony "Tony" Loria, Sr.

A few months after Carmine's indictment, Queen Bee got caught up, becoming a co-conspirator in the drug trafficking trial of Vincent Papa, Sr. The jury found him guilty on conspiracy to traffic in narcotics and the substantive offense of possession with intent to distribute 160 pounds of heroin, worth tens of millions of dollars.

Vincent Papa, Sr. was a major operator in the supply and distribution of heroin into New York City and Long Island. It was rumored that he moved an average of 25 kilos of heroin a week, an incredible sum. Then there were the rumors he was the mastermind behind the French Connection case. Between 1969 and 1972, 398 pounds of heroin and 120 pounds of cocaine—narcotics with a street value of $70 million— was stolen from the New York City Police Department's property clerk's office in lower Manhattan. It led to the dismantling of the Special Investigation Unit (SIU) of the NYPD Narcotics Division, the most corrupt law enforcement agency in American history.[34] Papa's story would inspire films like *The French Connection*[35] with Gene Hackman and *Prince of the City*[36] with Treat Williams.

---

[33] Wikipedia contributors, "Carmine Tramunti," Wikipedia, The Free Encyclopedia, https://en.wikipedia.org/w/index.php?title=Carmine_Tramunti&oldid=905873872 (accessed December 2, 2019).

[34] (32b) Jones, Thom L. "The Man Who Stole The French Connection." Gangsters Inc., 2 May 2011, http://gangstersinc.ning.com/profiles/blogs/the-man-who-stole-the-french

[35] The French Connection, Directed by William Friedkin, Philip D'Antoni Productions, 1971. Film.

[36] Prince Of The City, Directed by Sidney Lumet, Orion Pictures, 1981. Film

In 1975, Vincent Papa, Sr. was convicted and sent to a federal prison in Atlanta, Georgia. Two years later, he was murdered in prison, stabbed repeatedly by three black inmates with homemade knives, commonly known as shanks. Word had gotten out that Vincent Papa, Sr. cooperated in the SIU case. Papa, Sr. only informed on crooked cops—never the family. It was bad luck that the cops had mob connects, but in the criminal underworld snitching is snitching and a rat is a rat.

Papa, Sr.'s heroin organization had been structured along the lines of a typical American enterprise. The company had stationery with a personalized logo—a paper bag overflowing with bound stacks of fifty-and one-hundred-dollar bills. The stationery listed Vincent Papa, Sr. as the founder, owner, chief executive officer, and chairman of the board of directors. Because a heroin organization, like any other, requires both wholesale and retail marketing, the letterhead listed Queen Bee as vice-president for retail marketing/Harlem region. It was right there in print.

Joan "Queen Bee" Moreland is described in George Wallance's *Papa's Game* as an excitable black woman, college educated, in her early forties.[37] Queen Bee was a large woman with huge breasts, thick thighs and waist, and an oval face. She wore only white dresses, white shoes, and white stockings, a hangover from her days as a nurse, and always carried a pocketbook big enough to hold two .38 handguns. Queen Bee had been running card games in Harlem, making $500 a week, but she wanted more. She went to two of Vincent Papa, Sr.'s lower-level wholesalers and said she had $750 to purchase drugs.

"We don't do business that small," they told her.

---

[37] Wallance, Gregory J. Papa's Game. New York: Rawson, Wade Publishers; 1st edition 1981.

"Give me a chance. I can prove that I can do better," Queen Bee pleaded.

Papa, Sr.'s lieutenants relented and supplied her with eighth, quarter, and half kilograms of heroin, selling to her at an average price of $50,000 a kilo. Queen Bee's profit came from diluting the heroin with milk and sugar, or a substance called *bonita*, before it was sold to addicts. Queen Bee experimented with different proportions of milk, sugar, and heroin until she found a combination that made her addicts feel good, but allowed a maximum profit, at $1,500 to $2,000 an ounce.

Wallance alleged that Queen Bee was so brazen and ambitious, she even used her five children, ages six through twelve, as mules. They'd pick up the drugs from Papa Sr.'s men, drop them at one of the several apartments she stored the dope, and made home deliveries to dealers.[38] Children in the neighborhood were drawn to Queen Bee like she was the Pied Piper—she was charming, with a maternal nature despite her profession. On Halloween, the first place the kids stopped on the block was her apartment, as she was generous with candy and money. As a result, Queen Bee had an army of small, fast, and loyal employees to do her bidding.

The Southern District prosecutors would eventually turn Queen Bee, along with several key members of Vincent Papa, Sr.'s organization.

---

[38] Dembart, Lee. "3 Businessmen Arrested on Heroin Charges." The New York Times Archives, 3 March 1977, Page 25, https://www.nytimes.com/1977/03/03/archives/3-businessmen-arrested-on-heroin-charges.html

THE EX-NURSE WHO ONCE RAN Harlem's drug operations, secretly worked out a deal with prosecutors. She would eventually do less than five years behind bars. In board outline, the proof at trail based on Queen Bee's testimony, would reveal that Papa, Sr. was the top link, the director and source of supply (United States of America v. Vincent Papa, 533 F.2d 815 (2nd Cir. 1976)). The next line, working directly below Papa, Sr., was at various times, three wholesalers and co-defendants Anthony Stanzione, Victor Euphemia, and Jack Locorriere. It was testified that these men made deliveries to Queen Bee, who was a large retailer and served with her associates to link the heroin to Harlem's addict population. The wholesalers, at times, also used the services of "stash men", one of whom was Joseph Ragusa, who would, in turn deliver the heroin to Queen Bee. The trial records indicated this chain operated in New York City between 1967-1972.

Queen Bee occupied her functional level from the inception of the conspiracy charged to Papa, Sr. In 1967, Queen Bee was introduced to Euphemia and Stanzione, who were then acting in partnership during that year and continuing into 1968. They jointly served to supply Queen Bee through deliveries in Manhattan. Despite Euphemia and Stanzione's association dissolving sometime in 1968, each of them independently worked out deals with Queen Bee. The record went on to show that Stanzione furnished Queen Bee with heroin on a continuous basis through October 1969, making deliveries at several of Queen Bee's apartments in Manhattan or at Stanzione's home or business, both of which were located in the Bronx. Euphemia's independent dealings with Queen Bee continue through December 1969 and occurred at various Manhattan locations.

Queen Bee continue to testify that in December of 1969 Euphemia teamed up with Locorriere, who was the operator of Ditmar's Private Car Service in Astoria, Queens, and who introduced Locorriere to her. Thereafter, upon Euphemia's instruction Locorriere and Queen Bee began doing business directly and they used the car service as the meeting place of contact. It was through the car service that Ragusa, who turned out to be another principle government witness, became involved in the narcotics network. Locorriere hired Ragusa to work as a driver at the car service in the latter part of 1969 or early 1970. Queen Bee testified that soon after Ragusa was hired the scope of his employment was expanded. She indicated that Ragusa agreed to stash and deliver heroin for Locorriere and was taught the art of cutting heroin by his employer. From the stashed heroin, Ragusa made deliveries to Queen Bee and periodically made heroin pick-ups in Queens to replenish his supply. Ragusa would then take some of the stashed heroin for himself to sale to Queen Bee as his own.

On December 31, 1970, Locorriere telephoned Ragusa at the car service, since then Locorriere was neither seen nor heard from. Nevertheless, Ragusa continued to sell the heroin he had remaining from the Locorriere stash to Queen Bee and embezzled some of the money intended for Locorriere which he collected from her. The record reflected that Ragusa then agreed with Euphemia that he would continue operating for Euphemia as he had for Locorriere. The agreement, however, lapsed early in 1971.

Around the time of the Ragusa-Euphemia agreement, Ragusa met Papa, Sr. a short time later, when he came to the car service to retrieve the money Ragusa embezzled on the Locorriere stash sales to Queen Bee. Ragusa agreed to repay the money in installments and made the first payment at that time. The link between Locorriere and Papa, Sr. as his supplier is thus evidenced by Papa, Sr.'s posture vis a vis Ragusa.

Ragusa failed to make additional payments to Papa, Sr. The two met again in January and agreed that Ragusa would work off the debt by stashing heroin for Papa, Sr. Papa, Sr. introduced Ragusa to Stanzione. Stanzione delivered 160 pounds (worth about 40 million) of heroin to Ragusa for storage in the latter's Long Island City home with the understanding, under instructions from Papa, Sr., that Stanzione would have access to the stash at all times. Ragusa, no longer trusted as a collection agent, was not to make any sales himself. Ragusa nevertheless surreptitiously sold some of the heroin in his custody to Queen Bee on his own account, which inevitably revealed more information about the operations and allowing Queen Bee seek out Ragusa for more supplies. Queen Bee testified that Ragusa responded with needing to get permission from "Vinnie" because "he's the boss. . ." Ragusa met with Papa, Sr. at the Astoria Colts Social Club in Queens, a gathering place for members of the conspiracy, and tried to arrange this additional sale to Queen Bee.

Meanwhile, Euphemia was supplying the Queen Bee account. At one point during the summer of 1971, Queen Bee was able to make an expected payment to Euphemia. Euphemia told her that she better get that money because if she did not "Vinnie" would have his head. With other evidence presented at trial, it was reasonable to infer that the reference to "Vinnie" was to Vincent Papa, and that Euphemia wholesaled heroin supplied by Papa, Sr.

On February 3, 1972, Papa, Sr. was arrested in the Bronx. At the time of arrest, he and his companion, Joseph DiNapoli, were in possession of a suitcase containing nearly $1,000.000. Shortly after the money was seized, Euphemia told Queen Bee "that his people had got hit hard for money."

◆

IN THE MID 1970S FOLLOWING her release from prison, Queen Bee gathered her family and rented three apartments in 109 West 112th Street from a well-known Harlem landlord named Pete McDougal. He was a fixture uptown; his name was in the Who's Who of people you want to know in Harlem. McDougal owned a lot of real estate in Harlem as well as one of the city's biggest excavation and demolition companies. J. McDougal Equipment Corp. provided jobs for minorities and built houses all over Harlem.

He also partnered with pro-basketball superstar Wilt Chamberlain and bought Small's Paradise from founder and owner, Edwin Alexander Smalls, back in 1961. It was one of the most successful and well-known nightclubs in Harlem's history, and was frequented by many famous movie stars, athletes, and politicians, and other black luminaries, including Malcolm X, Mary McLeod Bethune, Paul Robeson, Billie Holiday, Willie Mays, Wes Montgomery, and Millie Jackson. It was also where Sheila would later meet and have a short courtship with Kurtis Blow, the first commercially successful rapper and the first to sign with a major record label. "The Breaks" was a single from his 1980 self-titled debut album, and the first certified gold record rap song for hip-hop.

Queen Bee moved to the 4th floor, while Tangie her oldest niece, settled on the 3rd and her nephew TJ ended up on the 2nd floor with his mother. Once Queen Bee had become comfortable and gotten reacquainted with her surroundings, she set up shop and used TJ, a teen at the time, to help sell heroin in the building's lobby. Queen Bee still had an established clientele, so TJ had a flow of regular customers.

TJ enjoyed working for his favorite aunt Queen Bee—she was fun and always showed him a good time. TJ was looking to make his own way, working longer hours selling drugs and earning more money. Building 109 also came with other criminal activities, like a number spot. It was run by Dewey and Tommy, the cousins of Pete McDougal. There was also a small-time street hustler named Perry, who ran the numbers and acted as a lookout for cops. There was even a pit bull named Numbers, who started out as a guard dog for the number spot, and later became the 112th Street mascot.

TJ was raised up around all types of illegal activities, as well as hustlers and gamblers, so he was raised more by the streets than his family. That wasn't surprising, as his parents had been hustlers themselves. His father, nicknamed Kid, served in the Vietnam War and when he came home, he ran with Ellsworth "Bumpy" Johnson. Bumpy was a notorious and feared mob boss, a long-time gangster who controlled gambling and extortion operations in Harlem. He was also Madam St. Clair's chief enforcer.

At the start of the 20th century, Madam St. Clair ran numerous criminal enterprises in Harlem. Notably, she resisted the interests of the Mafia for several years after Prohibition ended; she continued to be an independent operator and her business never came under Mafia control. Bumpy inspired the film *Hoodlum* starring Laurence Fishburne, and in the 1930s became the main Harlem associate of Charles "Lucky" Luciano, the first official boss of the modern Genovese crime family.[39] People like this paved the way for illegal activities.

In 1976-77 Evelyn had moved with Richard out of the overcrowded projects and into 109 West 112th Street, a newly renovated tenement. Evelyn found permanent work and planned to stay in Harlem—she was done with the south. They moved into a two-bedroom apartment on the ground level, down the hall from

---

[39] Biography.com Editors. "Bumpy Johnson Biography." The Biography.com, A&E Television Networks, 3 December 2019, https://www.biography.com/crime-figure/bumpy-johnson.

the number spot. Despite the criminal activity, it was a quiet block between St. Nicholas and Lenox Avenue, and the siblings wouldn't learn about the spot for some time.

Richard's high school days had come and gone. It was time to put away childish things and be a man. His cousin Curtis wanted to travel the world and fly planes, so he enlisted in the Air Force. Rob and Richard drifted apart following Rob's mother's suicide—she'd jumped from their 12th-floor window in the St. Nicholas Projects. Danny enrolled in Baruch College in Manhattan but made time to hang out with Richard on 112th Street. They would become the best of friends and for a while, inseparable.

Going to college, working a 9 to 5, or joining Uncle Sam's army was not what Richard saw himself doing. He was a young man on a mission, determined to make his own money and be his own boss. Richard decided to go to the Garment District in midtown and purchase clothes at wholesale to sell at retail. It kept a few dollars in his pocket, but the long hours and slow turnaround on his profit was ultimately not worth the time he invested. After a long day on Harlem's streets peddling his merchandise, Richard would often see a well-dressed young man named TJ hanging in the lobby of 109, a few feet away from his apartment, counting stacks of money. Richard spent a week observing TJ and wondering where and how he was getting his money. He finally worked up the courage to ask him.

"I'm selling coke and dope for my aunt," TJ explained.

Richard was quiet for a moment. *I want in on some of that money*, he thought. TJ liked Richard and could see the wheels spinning in his head. TJ first helped increase Richard's revenue by purchasing designer knockoffs and no-name brand clothing like sweat suits, jeans, dress shirts, and socks. The clothes weren't TJ's style, but he was the new kid on the block and looking to make a friend.

For TJ, selling drugs without a partner or team had its pros and cons. TJ found that out early on, when a guy ten times his size came back to him complaining about the quality of the heroin he'd sold him earlier that day. Richard heard a commotion outside his door, burst into the hallway, grabbed the huge man, and threw him out of the building.

A week after TJ's confrontation, Richard was hanging out in the hall waiting for a storm to stop. It was raining too hard for Richard to sell his marked-up Garment District clothes on the street. TJ was safe and dry in the lobby, already set up and selling Queen Bee's drugs. Richard saw TJ and couldn't hide his frustration.

"All this rain, I ain't making no money today selling these clothes," Richard said, half to himself.

"Why don't you help me? I'll split the profits 50/50," TJ offered. TJ was eager to find allies. Everyone knew his aunt, Queen Bee, but TJ was looking to earn respect and stand on his own name in the drug game. Richard had a tall, athletic build, and looked a lot more intimidating than TJ. He knew Richard could protect them both. Richard's demeanor—his willingness to help others, his ease in putting himself on the front line to help people—made him seem open and reliable. TJ felt like he could trust him, so he took a chance on Richard without first consulting with his aunt.

A few days later she noticed that TJ was coming back to re-up more often than usual.

"You've been doing really good lately, moving that stuff, and bringing in that money," Queen Bee said. She believed in praise only when it was really due.

"The kid down on the first floor been helping me," TJ said. "Bring him upstairs. I want to meet him," she commanded.

TJ introduced Richard to his aunt, and within a week Richard had become his best friend and an extended member of their family. Richard would hang out with TJ at Queen Bee's house, where she taught Richard Intro to the Dope and Coke Game 101. TJ and Richard would sit at the large kitchen table and watch Queen Bee cut dope and coke. She became Richard's mentor, teaching him how to cut, pack, sell, and move drugs. She also showed him how to avoid cops and stickup kids.

Every night when they shut the business down, Queen Bee would have Richard and TJ pour ammonia throughout the apartment building to mask the smell of drugs and keep vagrants from hanging out in the lobby. Neighbors dared not complain— either they were benefiting from payoffs or helping with drug distribution. Regardless, no one wanted a problem with Queen Bee because people knew she was connected to the mob.

Richard turned out to be instrumental in Queen Bee's business. He helped TJ move the product faster than he had in weeks. TJ went from making $2,000 a week in profit to $10,000. Richard had a knack for selling—he was assertive and charismatic—which helped their business grow. Richard was a special kind of salesman; even if his drugs weren't good, he'd convince you to buy them. He had that kind of gift.

TJ and Richard now had so many customers that they needed more room to maneuver, so they set up shop outside. They sat in a hooptie, an old raggedy car, in the front of the building and sold their drugs. They would grind day and night. They'd hustle in the freezing cold and on some days Evelyn, oblivious to his drug activity, wouldn't see Richard until early morning when she was leaving for work. Richard hustled hard and liked the money he generated—it was a lot more money than he had ever made selling clothes. Pretty soon, Richard would be on the street before TJ, in front of 109 at 6:00 AM, ready to snatch up customers from the dealers across the street. Richard was a strategist, and soon came up with another way to increase their drug sales.

"We're going to take our profits, buy drugs from your aunt, and give it away," Richard explained. TJ thought he'd gone crazy.

Richard continued, "The customers will put the word out that we're giving it away. That's how we'll bring in new customers."

TJ was wary, but he trusted Richard.

By the time the sun set, there was a mob of more than 100 people lined up outside for freebies. They had to grind hard to get rid of them all before the cops showed up. They did, but word was out and the next day the crowd tripled in number. They coordinated lines around the corner, farther away from police attention.

Their days got much longer as more people showed up. The lines kept forming; their hours were endless. Richard and TJ started wearing gloves because of all the money and people they had contact with. By the end of every night, the gloves were filthy. But the venture was worth it: The $10,000 they used to make in a week turned into $30,000, then doubled to $60,000.

"We gonna own the eighties," Fritz declared. "Everybody in Harlem is gonna owe me."

"Okay, whatever you say," TJ responded.

Everything Fritz said had come true. He would speak things into existence and TJ believed what he said.

Richard was a natural. He was good at selling drugs, and it allowed TJ to scale back his hours to run other errands for his aunt. Richard had help from his old high school buddy Danny. Queen Bee often trusted Danny to chaperone her to Washington Heights to re-up her drug supply. It was a big deal, and a sign that she trusted Danny to meet her connect. Besides that, he was a college boy who looked nonthreatening, and using his car made it convenient to transport drugs around. Everything seemed to be going well, and Queen Bee and Richard were happy with the large profits.

CHAPTER SIX

The Boogeyman Under The Bed

While Richard was growing his drug business, he had no clue that Sheila, Junior, and their new brother TyRay lived only a few train stops away in the Bronx. They were unhappy children, still living in a physically and mentally abusive environment, believing there was no way out. Danger for them was never more than a few feet away.

Sheila prayed every day for things to get better. She prayed for Elizabeth to walk through the front door and take them away from LeRoy. She prayed for Wilhelmina to sober up, gather her children, and leave. Sheila never imagined her situation could get any worse than the beatings and verbal abuse she endured. But it could.

While most girls start showing signs of puberty at around twelve or thirteen years old, Sheila started at about seven years old. She sprouted body hair quickly and skipped training bras altogether. Sheila always kept the bathroom door closed when she bathed but never felt the need to lock it until one day when she was eight years old—LeRoy came in without knocking, then stood over Sheila and watched her as she bathed. It was creepy, but what he did next was even viler.

LeRoy bent down, fondled Sheila's breast, then left the bathroom like nothing had happened. *Did he just touch me?* Sheila thought. She almost couldn't believe it had happened. She knew what he did wasn't right, but was too young to know how to react. Sheila didn't even finish bathing. She hurried out of the bath and put her PJs on. Sheila was confused and afraid. She took extra precaution when leaving the bathroom, peeking out to make sure LeRoy was not around.

Sheila hurried to the kitchen to get something to drink. LeRoy surprised her when he came into the room suddenly. She turned to him and froze, not sure what he would do next. He warned her not tell anyone about what happened in the bathroom. Sheila didn't understand what was happening or why. Why would he touch her like that? She knew that no grown man should ever touch a child's private areas. Until recently, she didn't even notice LeRoy checking her out in that way. He was an old man to her, and he made her feel unclean and self-conscious.

Sheila wanted to protect herself and was mindful of how she dressed around the house. She wore long sleeves and pants, hoping she could avoid LeRoy's attention. If keeping her mouth closed meant LeRoy would never touch her again, then she was willing to do just that.

A week later, LeRoy came into their bedroom. He and Wilhelmina had a fight and she drank herself to sleep. He was so quiet that Sheila didn't realize he was in the bedroom, until Sheila felt LeRoy's fingers on her leg and crawling up between her thighs. Sheila was in excruciating pain, too scared to move or scream out. Sheila didn't know what he was doing, she just wanted him to stop. Even though LeRoy wasn't their biological father, the children always addressed him as Dad.

"Dad why you doing this?" Sheila pleaded.

"Sh-h-h," LeRoy whispered, putting a finger to his lips.

LeRoy didn't want Sheila to wake up Junior and TyRay. When he finished doing his dirty deed he left. Sheila felt sticky and filthy between her legs. When she went to the bathroom to clean herself off, there were spots of blood on the washcloth. The next night LeRoy came, and the next night after that. He was getting bolder and staying longer, doing more things to Sheila. She thought having TyRay sleep in the bed with her might stop him, but he would simply pick up the baby and put him in the bed with Junior or Wilhelmina.

"Remember, this is between us," LeRoy said every time he came into the bedroom and violated Sheila.

Sheila kept the secret to herself for a while and never told Junior, but thought he saw LeRoy molest her one night. They shared the same room, how could he not? Junior slept on the top of the bunk bed and could see everything down below. LeRoy may have thought the same thing, because he abruptly stopped coming into the bedroom. LeRoy would wake Sheila up and tell her to come into the bathroom. Wilhelmina was sick, unable to get out of bed most of the time, and never knew what was going on.

In 1969, Wilhelmina was diagnosed with cancer. Sheila didn't even know what cancer was until she became very ill. Sheila was not sure if it was the cigarettes that gave her the cancer, but she'd go through a pack a day. Sheila didn't understand addiction at 12 years old, but she knew that Wilhelmina had to have cigarettes. On Christmas Day the year before, the snow was deep and the temperature extremely cold. Wilhelmina got Sheila and Junior up early and dressed to go to the store, so they could wait with her until it opened and she could buy more cigarettes.

Not long after Wilhelmina got cancer, she had to be hospitalized for several weeks. When she returned home she'd had three fingers amputated and was addicted to pain meds. The medication and drinking kept Wilhelmina in the bed or walking around the house like a zombie, oblivious to LeRoy's behavior.

The cancer didn't stop the domestic violence. If LeRoy had a bad day and was drinking heavily, he'd beat Wilhelmina like she was a stranger who had stolen something from him. He would punch her in the stomach and face. He would then kick and stomp her while she lay sprawled out and unresponsive. After he'd leave the house, Sheila would help Wilhelmina up off the floor and clean her up. At that point Sheila thought it was the perfect time to tell her about LeRoy molesting her. Sheila was sure that after Wilhelmina heard what she had to say, they'd be packed and gone before LeRoy came back.

"Mom, let's leave," Sheila said.

"LeRoy didn't mean to hurt me," Wilhelmina said.

"But he does it all the time and he hurts me too," Sheila blurted out.

"What you mean, he hurt you?"

"He comes in my room at night... and touches me."

"You're a fucking liar," Wilhelmina said, pulling away from Sheila. "I'm not lying!"

"He's not doing nothing to you. Shut up and go to your room!"

Sheila couldn't believe Wilhelmina called her a liar. Why would she make up a story like that? Why couldn't Wilhelmina see the fear on her face? *And shouldn't she know, as an adult, that I wouldn't lie about this?* she thought. Sheila was never an attention seeker. She was respectful, cared for Wilhelmina and her brothers, and did as she was told, but none of that mattered. Wilhelmina didn't believe Sheila and if she didn't, no one would. Sheila was on her own and had a secret she had to keep to herself for now.

LeRoy was worse than a monster—he was a savage, twisted and unstable, a child molester and sexual predator. Sheila was nine years old when he first stole her virginity; it felt like her insides were being ripped apart. Every time after that when LeRoy raped her, the pain was unbearable. Sheila felt like she was being tortured. She'd rather be hit with an iron cord every day than to experience such brutality, but she was powerless to stop him.

The first time he assaulted Sheila, Junior was in school and Wilhelmina was at a doctor's appointment with TyRay. She had a stomachache and had been throwing up in school all morning. The teacher called home and LeRoy picked her up. When they got home and he opened the door, there was an eerie silence. The house was empty and no one was home. Sheila wanted to run, but there was nowhere to go. "Oh God," Sheila whispered, hoping LeRoy didn't hear. She assumed, since she was sick and sent home from school with a possible stomach virus, LeRoy would give her a break.

"Go in the bathroom and wash up, so you can relax," LeRoy said. Sheila went straight into the bathroom, took off her soiled clothes, bathed, and put on her PJs. Then she went into her bedroom to lay down.

"Sheila, come here," LeRoy yelled from the living room.

Sheila put the blankets over her head and pretend not to hear him. "Sheila, I said come here!"

Sheila dragged herself out the bed and went into the living room and stood in the doorway. LeRoy was sitting on the couch watching television.

"Why you standing so far away? Come here, sit down," LeRoy said.

Sheila walked closer. LeRoy unbuttoned her PJ top, pushed

her back on the couch, and lay on top of her. It felt like she was being suffocated by his body weight. It was hard to breathe and she couldn't move, but she felt him unzip his pants, then there was a lot of pressure and pain between her legs.

"Ow!" Sheila yelled.

LeRoy covered her mouth with his hand. "Relax. I'm not going to hurt you," he said.

But he *was* hurting her. Sheila was hot and sweating. She felt nauseous and faint. She thought she passed out because the next thing she remembered she was standing up and facing LeRoy with her head down. Sheila couldn't look him in the face. She knew what he did wasn't right, but blamed herself and was ashamed she'd let it happen. She was feeling weak and sore between her legs. There was blood and liquid running down her thighs.

Leroy put his hands on Sheila's shoulders. "I need you to keep this between us," LeRoy said again. Sheila nodded.

"Go clean yourself up," LeRoy said.

Sheila could feel the nausea coming on again and before she could turn away from LeRoy she threw up all over him.

"What the fuck is you throwing up for?" LeRoy yelled, then he slapped Sheila so hard she fell down on the floor. "Now clean that shit up."

LeRoy was furious because he had to wash up and change his clothes before picking up Wilhelmina and TyRay from the doctor's office. When LeRoy went to the bathroom Sheila put on her PJs and wiped up the mess.

"Sheila!" LeRoy shouted from the bathroom.

When Sheila thought the day couldn't get any worse, it did. He was standing in the bathroom washing his member over the sink.

"Hold this for me," LeRoy said.

"I don't want to," Sheila said, shaking her head.

What's wrong with this man? Sheila thought. *What have I done wrong, that he feels the need to punish me like this?* She was just a child, and very confused. Her childhood had become one long nightmare.

LeRoy grabbed Sheila by the collar and pulled her to the sink. She did what he asked and he showed her how to use her hands to arouse him again. She stood frightened and still like a statue. She couldn't move. Her legs felt like they were cemented to the ground. Her arms were stiff, stretched out over the sink. Her hands felt clammy and gross. Sheila wanted to wash them, but she dared not move.

LeRoy washed himself off and brushed past her out of the bathroom. When Sheila heard the apartment front door close and lock, she was relieved. She put her hands down and looked at herself in the mirror and talked to God.

"I believe in you, God. But why are we going through this? What did we do?" Sheila wanted to die. She wanted to commit suicide. She wanted to slash her wrists or swallow a bunch of pills. It was the perfect opportunity and no one was home to stop her.

When they lived with Elizabeth and Claude they went to church regularly. Sheila was taught that suicide was a sin in the eyes of God and she'd go straight to hell if she did it. *Could hell really be worse than this?* Sheila thought. She then thought about her brothers.

Who would look after them if she killed herself? She knew it would be a selfish act, no matter what she was suffering.

Sheila washed her hands in the sink then undressed and took a bath. When she was finished she put on a fresh pair of PJs, got into bed, and cried. An hour or so later she heard voices at the front door. LeRoy, Wilhelmina, Junior, and TyRay were home. She stopped crying and wiped the tears off her face before Junior entered the bedroom.

"I heard you were sick in school today. You all right?" Junior asked.

"Yeah. I just have a stomachache," Sheila said.

Sheila never mentioned to Junior or Wilhelmina what happened that day. What she suffered for the next five years would've killed most people, but Sheila had other loved ones to consider.

CHAPTER SEVEN

Escape From The Boogeyman

WHILE SHEILA, JUNIOR, AND TYRAY were living with Wilhelmina and LeRoy, Elizabeth would stop by and check on them. During those times LeRoy either wasn't home or on his best behavior. Elizabeth knew that Wilhelmina and LeRoy would argue, but she had no idea the extent of abuse in the house.

When Sheila started having her period at seven years old, Wilhelmina monitored it on a wall calendar. Sheila was late one month when she was thirteen and Wilhelmina was concerned. She was unaware that LeRoy was having sex with her child and assumed that at her young age, it was impossible for her to be sexually active and pregnant. Wilhelmina rarely went anywhere unless LeRoy took her and he was at work, so Elizabeth took Sheila to the doctor.

Sheila was uncomfortable and nervous to find out that Elizabeth had taken her to a male gynecologist. The thought of a man touching her, even a doctor, made her uneasy. Because of her age Elizabeth needed to be in the exam room with her. Before Sheila undressed for the exam, the gynecologist sat and talked about what to expect during the exam. The gynecologist's voice was calm and soothing, which made Sheila relax a little. She told the gynecologist about having pain with her period and heavy bleeding. The gynecologist wanted to do an internal pelvic exam. Elizabeth helped her out of her clothes and she put on the paper robe. She laid back on the exam table, put her feet in the metal stirrups, and stared at the white cork ceiling. She tried to relax by breathing slowly. The gynecologist put a sheet covering on her from the waist down and started his exam. The gynecologist was careful and gentle, but Sheila still felt dirty and embarrassed. Before finishing the exam, the gynecologist performed a Pap smear.

"Pap smear?" Elizabeth questioned.

"Yes, just a precaution," the he responded.

When he was done, the doctor and Elizabeth stepped out the exam room for a several minutes.

When they returned, Elizabeth's disposition had changed. She looked agitated and upset.

"Sheila, I'm going to ask you something and I need you to be honest with me," the gynecologist said.

"Okay," Sheila said.

"Did anybody touch you?" the gynecologist asked. "Touch me how?"

"Touched you where I just examined you."

"Baby, don't be afraid to tell the doctor," Elizabeth said. "No." Sheila shook her head.

The gynecologist knew by his exam that Sheila was sexually active, but he didn't want to force the issue, hoping she would tell them the truth in her own time. The doctor and Sheila talked about school, her friends, her siblings. He wanted to help, but his hands were tied without her statement, which would corroborate his findings. And Sheila was too frightened of what might happen if she told him about LeRoy. She didn't want to be taken away or separated from her siblings. She also didn't want Wilhelmina to get in trouble.

The gynecologist handed Elizabeth a card and left the examination room. Elizabeth helped Sheila put on her clothes and gave her a big hug.

"It's going to be all right, baby," Elizabeth said.

On the ride home Elizabeth was quiet. She knew Sheila was being forced into sex, but she felt helpless. If Sheila couldn't admit that she was being abused, charges couldn't be filed.

After their visit to the gynecologist, Elizabeth started dropping by unannounced. One weekend when she showed up, she found Junior with an eye swollen shut from LeRoy's latest beating. LeRoy wasn't home and Elizabeth went in on Wilhelmina.

"What the fuck is going on in here, Wilhelmina! This man is abusing you, abusing your children, and you're not saying or doing nothing?"

Elizabeth threatened to take Sheila, Junior, and TyRay away from their mother.

"You going to have to take me to court. These my children," Wilhelmina said.

They argued back and forth for a while. Elizabeth grabbed her bag to leave, then turned to Sheila. "Sheila, just hang in there a little while longer if you can," Elizabeth said, then she kissed all three children and walked out of the house, slamming the door behind her.

Sheila believed Elizabeth and tried her best to be good so there would be no problems. Sheila talked to Junior and told him to try to stay out LeRoy's way. Elizabeth knew that they weren't in good hands, but Wilhelmina was their mother, and legally Elizabeth couldn't just take Sheila and her brothers.

A few months after the gynecologist visit, LeRoy started having an affair with a woman in their neighborhood named

Janet. Sheila was relieved, because while he was seeing his mistress, he wasn't abusing her. But she felt bad for her mother when LeRoy brought Janet to the house. LeRoy would put his wife out of their bedroom and sleep with Janet in their bed. Sheila would hear Wilhelmina on the couch crying until she fell asleep. Wilhelmina would repeatedly tell LeRoy she was unhappy and wanted him to end the affair. He'd remind Wilhelmina that he paid the bills and could do what he wanted inside and outside of his house.

He then took the affair a step further and started bringing Janet and her two children over to spend the night. Her children shared a bed with Junior, while TyRay slept with Sheila.

One day Wilhelmina finally had enough and put her foot down with LeRoy. She picked herself up off the couch and went into their bedroom.

"LeRoy, I want you, this woman, and her children out my house tonight!"

The argument between LeRoy and Wilhelmina was loud that night. Wilhelmina finally started to voice what she knew was wrong. Sheila was proud and scared for her at the same time. Proud she was speaking up for herself but scared of LeRoy's rage. Wilhelmina knew there would be consequences, but she didn't care.

She took a brutal beating that night. LeRoy beat her in front of Janet. Wilhelmina's hair was long, down her back. LeRoy grabbed her by the hair and twisted it tight around one hand while he beat her with the other. Sheila stood there and watched him beat her mother. There was nothing she could do. Sheila looked at him and wondered how someone could have so much hate in them, could be this cruel. Wilhelmina was a light-skinned woman, and her face turned black and blue from LeRoy's fists. Then he dragged her by her hair to the kitchen, where he took a knife to her hair. LeRoy left Wilhelmina on the floor, her hair scattered all around her. Wilhelmina got her point across though, because LeRoy gathered his mistress and they all left in the middle of the night.

Now was the time for their escape. Sheila kneeled and wiped Wilhelmina's face with a wet towel and tried to help her up off the floor.

"Let's go, Mom. We need to get to Elizabeth's house," Sheila said. Wilhelmina refused to leave. *Did she feel too old to be starting all over again?* Sheila wondered. Wilhelmina's children were by two different men, maybe she felt her family was too much baggage. Maybe it was because LeRoy Walker was the only man she had ever been with besides Clifford Harrison. Sheila didn't know the answer, but she knew her mother still loved LeRoy and believed he would change, despite everything he had done to them. There was nothing Wilhelmina wouldn't do for LeRoy. It astonished Sheila how she could stay with him, allowing him to abuse her and her children. Sheila knew Wilhelmina wasn't a bad person, but she needed help that she wouldn't seek.

That night was the first time Sheila saw Wilhelmina, *really* s aw her. Sheila looked at her mother, the sadness in her eyes, the blood and bruises on her face. *Who is this woman?* Sheila wondered. She didn't recognize Wilhelmina anymore.

At that moment, something came over Sheila. She refused to subject herself and her brothers to the abuse any longer. Sheila got off her knees with bloodstained hands and clothes. She was afraid and her mind raced with thoughts about her next move. *Do I take my siblings and go?* Sheila wondered.

She knew she needed to move fast before LeRoy came back home. Sheila decided it was time to get the hell up and out of there. She hurried to the bedroom, woke Junior and had him dress TyRay. Sheila then grabbed a few of their things from the closet and dresser, all she could carry in a small overnight bag. She took underclothes, a clean outfit for each of them, baby bottles, and diapers.

Then she retrieved a cigarette box she'd hid in the bottom of her bedroom closet. In it she'd saved every dollar Elizabeth had given her over the years, more than $1,000. Sheila put the cigarette box under one arm, the bag across her shoulder, and with TyRay on her waist, Junior and Sheila headed to the front door, leaving Wilhelmina behind.

It was late and the street was dark and empty. Sheila grabbed Junior's hand and hurried up the block, looking ahead, hoping not to see LeRoy driving back to the house. They reached the end of the block and tried to hail a taxi.

"You think we going make it to Elizabeth's house?" Junior asked. "Yeah, we will," Sheila said sounding surer than she felt.

It took them a long time to get a cab at that time of night, but one finally stopped and they climbed in. The taxi driver looked at them strangely. Sheila could only imagine what he was thinking, two children and a toddler flagging down a cab at one in the morning.

"Where ya going?"

Sheila gave him Elizabeth's address in Harlem.

The taxi driver drove off, and when Sheila was sure the taxi driver was not peeking through his rearview mirror at them, she took twenty dollars out of her cigarette box. Sheila held onto the money until it was time to pay. Halfway there TyRay started to cry because he was cold. Sheila put her arms around him and kept him warm with her body heat to quiet him. Sheila didn't want the taxi driver putting them out or asking questions about where their parents were.

They finally reached Elizabeth's house. Sheila paid the driver and they ran upstairs and banged on the door. When Elizabeth opened it, she looked at Sheila, Junior, and TyRay, bewildered.

"Where's your mother?" Elizabeth asked, leading them inside. "LeRoy beat her up again. We can't do this no more, Grandma," Sheila said, then burst into tears.

Claude walked into the living room, saw them half-dressed in the middle of the night, heard what happened, and was livid. Claude was tired of Wilhelmina and ready to go to the Bronx and kill LeRoy. Sheila helped Elizabeth make a bed for her brothers and tuck them in. Sheila then sat down with Elizabeth and Claude, and told them everything: about the mistress, the beatings, and the sexual assault.

"Did you tell your mother LeRoy was touching you?" Elizabeth asked. She and her husband were deeply distressed over what they'd been told.

"Yes, but Mom didn't believe me."

"What you want to do?" Claude asked. His mouth was set in a hard line.

"I don't want to go back there," Sheila said.

Elizabeth and Claude assured Sheila that they were safe and promised that they never had to go back to that house. Then the telephone rang. It was Wilhelmina crying and pleading for Elizabeth to bring the children back, that they were her children, and they didn't have the right to keep them. Sheila knew this wasn't Wilhelmina talking—it was LeRoy in her ear.

Wilhelmina's pleas fell on deaf ears. Elizabeth didn't want to hear what she had to say and was unconcerned about threats.

"I'll take you to court before you take me," Elizabeth said, and hung up the telephone.

LeRoy was bold—the next day he came to the Robinsons' house. Junior and Sheila were playing on the front stoop, where Elizabeth could keep an eye on them from the window. LeRoy pulled up in his car and demanded that the children get in. Claude saw LeRoy and grabbed his pearl-handled revolver out of the china cabinet. He and Elizabeth then ran outside like grizzly bears protecting their cubs.

"Mrs. Robinson, I came to get the children," LeRoy said.

Elizabeth didn't back down. "You ain't come to get a got damn soul here. What you do in the Bronx, you can't do down here," she said.

"Y'all children go upstairs now!" Claude demanded.

Junior and Sheila ran upstairs like they were told and never looked back. Sheila knew her grandparents could handle LeRoy; she wasn't worried anymore.

LeRoy felt he had a right to take TyRay because he was his biological child. Claude didn't care; the only way LeRoy was taking any of them back to the Bronx was over his dead body. They were in Harlem to stay.

Sheila thanked God for Elizabeth. She saved their lives that day. Wilhelmina didn't have a strong maternal instinct, and both the cancer and LeRoy had beaten her down. Sheila didn't blame her mother for the hell she and her brothers went through in that house. Neither did she blame her for the lack of encouragement, comfort, and protection. Sheila was able to forgive her because Elizabeth gave them those things and so much more. Sheila learned how to pack the bad stuff away. She figured there would be a day she would have to face it all head on, but it wouldn't be anytime soon.

CHAPTER EIGHT

The Boogeyman Come And Gone

Living with Elizabeth and Claude was good for Sheila and Junior and they got used to their new normal. The children had survived a lot of mental and physical damage, but they felt safe.

Meanwhile, family members were in Elizabeth and Claude's ear that they didn't want Wilhelmina's problems. They felt Sheila, Junior, and TyRay were baggage, and at their age they didn't want the responsibility of three more mouths to feed. Elizabeth and Claude let their negative comments fly over their heads and kept their hearts and home open to their grandchildren, who needed their support and protection. They were old school and family always came first regardless of the circumstances.

Elizabeth and Claude were true Christians, kind, loving, and giving to family and community. Elizabeth would take food out of her own refrigerator to feed neighbors who were hungry. She'd send them home with shopping bags filled with bread, meat, vegetables, and fruit. If a neighbor came knocking on Elizabeth's door in need a few dollars, she'd give it to them without question. The children saw her do this many times.

There were many seniors in the building who were disabled, unable to cook for themselves, and had no family around to help them. Elizabeth would often spend her entire disability check to prepare breakfast and lunch in the community room for local seniors. She wouldn't turn her back on anyone, that's just who she was. She believed everybody deserved help, and everybody deserved a second chance. Sheila often heard her grandmother say that as many times as God forgives, we should do the same.

Sundays with the Robinsons was like the movie *Soul Food*[40] now that the children lived there. There was lots of laughter, good food, and love. Claude was the executive chef in his five-star kitchen and sometimes the children were his sous chefs. The spread was big with all kinds of dishes: roast chicken, barbecue ribs, pot roast, macaroni and cheese, red rice, yams, collard greens, string beans with smoked turkey, cornbread, dinner rolls, cake, and pie.

Claude was hardworking and well-liked by the work crew on his job site. When he fell ill and couldn't work for several weeks the construction foreman, a big brawny Italian man, handed Claude a check to hold him and his family down until he returned to work. When Claude retired, he'd get up early like he still had a 9 to 5, take Elizabeth to work, then come back, cook a hot breakfast, and get the older kids ready for school and TyRay for the babysitter. He'd even comb Sheila's hair. The part was crooked, but the ponytails were perfect. After school when they came home the snacks were out, dinner cooking and ready to eat after Claude checked their homework. Before he'd pick Elizabeth up from work in the

---

[40] Soul Food, Directed by George Tillman Jr., Fox 2000 Pictures, 1997. Film.

evening, he made sure the children were bathed and had their PJs on. Sheila and her brothers thrived under their grandparents' care and concern. Watching Elizabeth and Claude's partnership also created a road map for the children on what a healthy relationship between a couple looked like.

Claude was a true patriarch and old school, which meant different rules for boys and girls. For Sheila, this meant no red lipstick or nail polish, no chewing and popping bubble gum—this was the stuff of jezebels. He thought children should speak only when spoken to and stay out of grown folk business. He didn't have a problem giving a child an ass whupping for being disrespectful around him.

Sheila never got a beating from him because she caught on quick, even when it was difficult to follow his rules. He had taken Sheila, Junior, and TyRay into his home; she wasn't going to be a problem and TyRay was too young to be one. Junior—who had a lot of behavioral issues as a result of LeRoy's abuse—was another story.

Meanwhile, Wilhelmina's harassing of Elizabeth and Claude over bringing her children home became its own issue.

Wilhelmina's alcohol addiction got worse with each passing day after the children left the Bronx. She was binge drinking and out of control. She'd come to Elizabeth and Claude's home being disrespectful, getting into shouting matches over the children, demanding money they refused to give her to support her drinking. She'd bring LeRoy to family gatherings and community events to cause a scene and curse people out. It was embarrassing for the children to see their mother incoherent, slurring, and falling down, with all the neighbors looking and the children laughing.

Several weeks after Sheila and her brothers escaped the house of horrors, Wilhelmina and LeRoy came knocking on the Robinsons' door. Elizabeth, Claude, Sheila, Junior, and TyRay were in the living room enjoying a quiet evening. Elizabeth opened the door and Wilhelmina and LeRoy entered. They had both been drinking. When Wilhelmina gave her children a hug, the smell of liquor was strong from her pores it was like she'd bathed in it. Once again, she wanted her children to come back home. Sheila didn't want to go. She told her *no*.

"You not gonna tell me what you are and not going to do!" Wilhelmina said.

"Leave the child alone, Wilhelmina," Claude demanded.

"Ya muthafuckers tryin' to steal my children away from me," Wilhelmina yelled.

"Mommy, why are you disrespecting Grandpa like that," Sheila asked. "We want to stay here," she pleaded.

"How you gonna take care these children and you can't even take care of yourself. Look at you, you drunk," Claude said.

"These are my children," Wilhelmina repeated again and again.

"Come on ya," LeRoy said, stretching his arms out, coaching the children to come to him.

With an angry scowl Sheila planted her feet firmly on the parquet floor and shoved both Junior and TyRay behind her to shield them from LeRoy. They could tell by her tone and her body language that she wasn't afraid of him anymore.

Claude got off the couch and opened the front door. "Get the fuck out," he said to LeRoy. He turned to Wilhelmina. "And you can go with him."

"I ain't going nowhere without my children!" Wilhelmina shouted. Sheila stood firm. "I'm not going back there, ever."

"Oh yes you will," Wilhelmina snapped. She lunged at her daughter, slapping her across the face.

The slap on Sheila's cheek felt like a thousand bee stings. She instinctively reacted, and without thinking she slapped her mother right back.

"I told you to leave that girl alone," Claude said.

Sheila felt awful. It was a reflex and a reminder of the abuse she had escaped. Sheila loved Wilhelmina; no matter what, she was still her mother. But she was fed up and tired of all the drama Wilhelmina brought every time she visited. One minute they were her children and the next minute they weren't. It was confusing to her.

Elizabeth wasn't worried about Wilhelmina's threats to take her to court. She knew Wilhelmina wasn't ready to care for any children— she could barely take care of herself. She was in and out of psych wards after having a nervous breakdown, unable to function normally after the combination of Clifford's death, LeRoy's abuse, her cancer scare, and her children's dismissal. Elizabeth would not let her daughter take the children back, but she didn't turn her back on her, either. She loved too much.

Sheila had just returned home from a school trip. She'd had a good day and was smiling until she saw the ambulance outside Elizabeth and Claude's building. Sheila immediately thought it must have something to do with Wilhelmina. The feeling she had in her stomach told her the situation was serious. When she reached the building, she saw Claude coming out with EMS carrying Elizabeth on a stretcher. Her grandmother was covered in bright red blood.

The children would find out later that Wilhelmina had once again come over with LeRoy, and both had been drinking heavily. LeRoy started accusing Wilhelmina of cheating on him. One thing led to another, LeRoy pulled out a knife to stab Wilhelmina, and Elizabeth stepped in the way to protect her daughter. LeRoy, always a coward, ran off before the cops could arrest him. Wilhelmina never pressed charges and begged Elizabeth not to.

With his wife's stabbing, Claude reached the limit of his patience with Wilhelmina. He washed his hands of Wilhelmina once and for all and wanted Elizabeth to do the same. He loved his wife too much and didn't want to see any more harm come to her. But Elizabeth would never let her daughter go. No matter what Claude had to say, she'd walk through fire if she thought it would help her child.

In Harlem the only thing worse than a wine-o was a dope fiend. Unbeknownst to his family, Richard was indirectly contributing to the drug epidemic in Harlem, dealing heroin for Queen Bee.

One afternoon Sheila and a friend had gone on the roof in Sheila's grandparents' building to play. There they stumbled over her friend Chris' uncle with his pants around his ankles. He was shooting dope into his penis. They later learned that dope fiends shot up this way to hide drug use or as a last resort after their other veins had collapsed from overuse. The image gave Sheila chills. She knew that must hurt, but the need for heroin must hurt more. It was very upsetting.

Sheila didn't know she would use someone's addiction, a family member's sickness, to hurt a friend. But children always made fun of other children, and sometimes the teasing methods were cruel. It's partly why Sheila hated when Wilhelmina came to Harlem intoxicated, and acting a fool in the streets for everyone to see.

At 13 Sheila had grown a thick skin, because she had heard, seen, and endured things that forced her to mature much faster than other children. She was sharp and her mouth was too, so when someone came for her or Wilhelmina, she always knew how to come back strong. Junior's strategy was to fight anybody who said anything about their mother, but Sheila relied on her wits. She could shut it down and make children cry if they talked about Wilhelmina.

A week after Sheila saw her neighbor Chris' uncle on the roof shooting dope, Wilhelmina came around to visit the children. Sheila was outside playing with her friends. Wilhelmina was drunk and everyone knew it. Chris made a derogatory remark about Wilhelmina, and Sheila immediately brought out her ammunition.

"Your momma an alcoholic," Chris said.

"Your uncle a dope fiend," Sheila shot back. "I seen his ass on the roof last week, nodding, with a needle hanging from his dick. If you didn't know, your momma's brother's a fiend. I'ma tell it, now go tell your momma that," Sheila finished.

"You a liar!" Chris shouted.

"And your uncle a dope fiend," Sheila repeated. "Your momma a drunk."

"I'd rather my mom be a drunk than a junkie."

Chris walked away angry and defeated, as the children who'd gathered to watch laughed uncontrollably.

CHAPTER NINE

Harlem Boy Lost

Phencyclidine (PCP), also known as "angel dust," was another popular recreational drug used in the 70s.[41] Some of its side effects include hallucinations, severe mood disorders, amnesia, paranoia, and violent hostility. It was estimated at that time by federal authorities that there were over seven million users of PCP in the United States.[42]

Junior became one out of the seven million, but not willingly. Junior already had a lot of anger issues after years of abuse at LeRoy's hands. A few months after moving in with his grandparents Junior was admitted to the psych ward at Harlem Hospital, after unknowingly drinking a soda laced with PCP. The family believed

---

[41] L. Anderson, PharmD. "PCP (Phencyclidine)." Drugs.com, Commonly Abused Drugs and Substance, 24 April 2018, https://www.drugs.com/illicit/pcp.html.

[42] Schindehette, Susan. "Danger in the Dust." People.Com, Archive, 16 December 2002, https://people.com/archive/danger-in-the-dust-vol-58-no-25/.

this dosing had long-lasting side effects and contributed to Junior's behavioral issues and problems with the law and authority.

If Junior's father hadn't been murdered and Junior had grown up with his older brother Richard, maybe things would have been different. But like most children, Junior had no control over his environment—but he became a product of it nevertheless. He was in and out of mental institutions and Spofford Juvenile Detention Center several times throughout his teens. Spofford was an infamous intake facility in the Bronx. Around 95% of its detainees were black or Latino children from the same handful of low-income neighborhoods. It was eventually shut down for ethical violations.[43]

When Claude disciplined Junior, he didn't mean or want to hurt him but to teach him a lesson, get him to behave himself. But it didn't matter. The violence Junior had seen and suffered had made him immune to physical pain. Junior didn't cry because you were hurting him; he cried because he knew you wanted to hear crying.

One afternoon Junior and Sheila went uptown to a basketball game at Riverside Church. Following the game was an after-party in the cramped basement gym. Claude instructed them to be back home by eleven o'clock and not a minute after. Before going their separate ways at the party, Sheila and Junior coordinated a time and place where they would meet if they couldn't find each other so they'd make their curfew.

Sheila was having a good time, but as much as she wanted to stay, she left and waited for Junior outside at the designated area.

---

[43] Beekman, Daniel. "Bronx's notorious Spofford, aka Bridges Juvenile Center, finally shut down." New York Daily News. com, 31 March 2011, https://www.nydailynews.com/new-york/bronx/bronx-notorious-spofford-aka-bridges-juvenile-center-finally-shut-article-1.119333.

She waited and waited… but Junior was a no-show. Sheila didn't want to miss curfew and headed home. She got to their grandparents' building and Junior was not in front waiting as she'd hoped. Their grandparents occupied a 4th floor apartment with a front window. Sheila knew her grandmother would be looking out of the window for them, so she leaned as flat as she could into the brownstone's vestibule where she couldn't be seen from above. She waited for Junior as long as she could before running upstairs. She rang the bell and Elizabeth opened the door.

"Where's Junior?" she asked, looking down the hallway. "Didn't you two leave out here together?"

"Yes, but we split up when we went inside."

Junior didn't get home until 3:30 in the morning. This was the first time Claude put a belt to his ass. After Junior got through hooting and hollering, he came back in the room and didn't have a single tear in his eye.

"You see how easy that was," Junior boasted. For Junior, it was all about the chase. Sheila thought Claude would go into cardiac arrest, chasing Junior around the house and moving furniture trying to get to him.

Claude finally realized that the spankings and yelling were ineffective, so he tried to find constructive ways to channel Junior's anger and recklessness. He tried everything he could to give Junior a normal life and be a positive role model. He put Junior in karate classes, an art he would eventually master—and which ironically made him more dangerous. Claude signed him up with the Police Athletic League (PAL) and a community basketball team, and he taught him how to play chess and cards. If it would keep Junior out of trouble, off the streets, and focused on something positive, Claude got him involved. Junior sat around the house many days playing chess and card games with his grandfather and his friends. The men taught him how to play poker, bid whist, and blackjack. Junior loved to play cards: he was good at it, he liked to take chances, and it was a quick way to make an easy buck on the street.

It was a hot summer day, and Junior and Sheila had to go to 125th Street to pick something up for Claude. He gave Junior $100 to shop with. There was a small-time hustler who would play a card game on the street called three-card Monte. It was a short con in which a shill, also called a plant or a stooge, pretends to conspire with the mark to cheat the dealer, while in fact he is conspiring with the dealer to cheat the mark.

There was a crowd standing and cheering on a player winning money from a conman shuffling three cards on a cardboard box. Junior and Sheila stopped and watched him quickly shuffling around a queen of hearts with two other cards, trying to confuse the player about which card was which. The player picked the queen of hearts every time and kept winning; $10, $20, $40. The player's bankroll was getting thicker and thicker. Junior and Sheila didn't know that the player was a part of the con to lure the mark.

"Sheila, I'ma play," Junior said, hyped to win some money.

"Boy, come on," Sheila said. When he was slow to reply she said sternly, "Don't do it."

"Sheila, I got this," Junior said confidently.

Sheila backed away. "I want you to know I got nothing to do with this. So when you get in trouble, you need to express that real quick to Grandpa."

Junior shrugged and stepped up to the cardboard box. He started betting with Claude's money and very quickly won up almost $400 in a streak.

"Let's go, Junior," Sheila said, taking his arm and trying to steer him away from the table.

Junior pulled his arm away. "Sheila, I got this, one more time." The siblings went back and forth loudly.

"Are you going to play or talk?" the dealer finally interjected. He wasn't willing to lose customers over some kids.

"I'm gonna play," Junior insisted. He tossed a twenty-dollar bill on the table.

Sheila kept at him. "Junior, you keep this up I'm going to leave your ass right here."

"You lose," the dealer shouted and took the twenty.

"Go on Sheila, I'll catch up with you." Junior tossed forty dollars on the table.

"You lose again." The dealer scooped up the dollars.

"Ah man. Sheila, you are making me lose." Junior tried to get away from her. "You're messing up my flow with all that nagging." But he was unable to focus with all the fussing and going back and forth.

"Little man… you sure you want to do this?" the dealer asked. It would be his only warning.

"Hell yeah," Junior responded, his chest out as he tossed another forty on the table.

The dealer flipped the cards. "You lose again."

"Yeah, I see you got this," Sheila said sarcastically. "We can still walk away, and Grandpa will never know."

At this point Junior had tuned everyone out, including the dealer, Sheila, and the crowd. He closed his eyes and said a prayer, then placed five crispy twenty-dollar bills on the cardboard box.

"Keep your eyes on the queen," the dealer said, holding up the card. "The queen is the money card." The dealer flipped over the joker card for Junior to see, then flipped it facedown. "Remember the jokers don't pay. Keep your eyes on the queen, it could be your lucky day."

Junior was focused on the three cards as the dealer shuffled, then stopped.

Junior pointed to the card on the left. The dealer took five twenties and slammed them down on the card Junior chose, then flipped it over. It was the joker.

"You lose again," the dealer shouted, sliding Junior's money off the box.

"Damn boy, they got you too," laughed a bystander in the crowd.

Junior turned to Sheila with a look of defeat. "What we going do?" he asked, dumbfounded.

"*We?* You told me *you* had this."

Sheila left Junior standing there and ran back home to tell Grandpa what happened before Junior got there. Sheila was serious—she wanted no part of that ass-whupping Junior was gonna get.

Did he learn a valuable lesson that day? No, but he did discover a new get-rich-quick scheme and set up his own three-card Monte game on 125th Street. Later he took it to midtown. Junior liked taking risks, living on the edge. He bored easily, and gambling was exciting. Junior knew how to make money; he just didn't know how to keep it. Everything was a bet, and everybody was a mark. If there was a chance to make a buck off someone, he was going to find a way to get it. Sheila had the biggest room in their grandparents' apartment, and they were always playing Pitch and Toss against the walls. They'd take turns throwing a coin at a wall from some distance away, and the coin that landed closest to the wall was the winner. They played with pennies, nickels, dimes, and quarters. Junior was never happy unless he was the one walking away with a pocket full of coins.

A few weeks after the three-card Monte game Junior did something more stupid. One night when Elizabeth and Claude were out, Junior took the key to the china cabinet off their bedroom dresser and removed the .22 pearl-handled revolver Claude hid there. Junior started posing with the revolver in a mirror, trying to look cool.

"Put that gun back," Sheila said. "In a minute," Junior replied.

"If Grandpa catch you with that gun you know what's gonna happen," Sheila warned him.

She walked out of the room and didn't think about it again. Sheila had seen Junior lock the cabinet and assumed he'd put the revolver back.

Three days later Claude wanted to speak to Sheila and Junior together.

"I had a revolver in the china cabinet. *I want to know who the hell went in my drawer and took my pistol out of the cabinet?*" he asked.

"It wasn't me," Sheila said.

Junior stood there and said nothing.

"I'm waiting on you to say something, Junior," Claude said. When he didn't answer he looked at Sheila. "Did you see him take the revolver?"

Sheila hated being around when Junior did dumb shit. They would always ask her what happened, and it put her in a bind. She didn't like lying to her grandparents or getting her brother in trouble. But Claude was determined to find out what happen to his gun, and Junior was slow to respond, so Sheila spoke up.

"I did see him with the revolver, but he put it back," Sheila said. "Where did he get the key from?" Claude asked.

"I don't know," Sheila answered.

He asked Junior the same question. "I found it on the table," Junior said.

"Now you lying to me," Claude said and popped Junior in the mouth. " Why didn't you put my pistol back?"

After a few minutes of staring at the floor the truth finally came out. Junior had been gambling and a guy tried to cheat him after losing. Junior got the gun to scare the guy into paying, but while he was brandishing the gun he saw police and threw it down the nearest sewer drain. Claude made Junior take him to the sewer but they couldn't find the gun. Then he took Junior home and beat his ass good.

Harlem was losing too many young black men to drugs and prison. Claude refused to allow his grandson Junior become a statistic on the streets. He believed if he taught Junior how to be an entrepreneur, he could make an honest living, give him self-worth, and as always, keep him out of trouble.

Claude had a fishing buddy named Benny, who could only communicate through a tube attached to his trachea—a consequence of a bad smoking habit. Claude convinced Benny to partner with him on a fruit and vegetable stand and have Junior run it. Claude and Benny traveled to Hunts Point in the South Bronx, one of the largest food distribution centers in the world. There they were able to buy a variety of fruits and vegetables wholesale. They helped Junior with the setup and pricing. Things were going well with the stand; they were making money and customers were happy. Even better, Junior was motivated, showing leadership skills and responsibility.

One day Claude let Junior run the stand without supervision. Later that day, he sent Sheila to check on him. Junior was gone and the stand was closed. Junior had made $500 in sales that day and gambled it all away. Claude was furious and when Junior came home, he asked no questions and went to whupping him the minute he walked through the door.

"No, no, no, you about to kill this boy. Don't beat him no more!" Elizabeth shouted as she stepped between the belt and Junior.

Junior was getting older: there was a state prison cell waiting with his name on it now, no more juvenile detention. Sheila knew that day would come, but never thought it would be for murder.

It was the summer of 1976. Junior went to hang out with his best friend, Calvin. He hadn't seen him for a while and found out he was being bullied and was afraid to play at P.S. 92. He was hiding at home, a quiet kid who never started trouble.

"Get your clothes on and let's go outside," Junior told Calvin.

Calvin got dressed and they walked to the schoolyard. Deebo, a local bully, immediately ran up on them and threatened Calvin.

"What's the problem?" Junior asked.

"Mind your business. This got nothing to do with you," Deebo said to him.

"This is my business and my friend," Junior said.

A few more words were exchanged between the two, then Deebo strutted away. Junior knew he hung out in the St. Nicholas Projects. Later that day he went over there by himself to confront him. He had hoped to stop Deebo from harassing his friend, but one thing led to another. They started fighting and Junior choked him out with his bare hands, killing him. He left the boy's body on a bench in the projects and ran.

When Junior came home his shirt was torn and bloody. He asked Sheila to put the shirt in a bag and throw it downstairs in the garbage. She did what he asked, because her main concern was that they not cause any trouble for their grandparents. Sheila never asked what happened to him—she was afraid what Junior would say. She'd find out a few days later though, when detectives came knocking on the door to take him away. He would do several years behind bars for the crime.

Sheila, Junior, and TyRay's escape from LeRoy's house of horrors seemed part of a distant past, but they all suffered from the long-term effects of the abuse. TyRay was the lucky one, he was too young to really remember his father's violence. Sheila was able to get through the horrors by being a constant caretaker for her mother and brothers. It meant she didn't have to focus too much on her own health and the abuse. She was determined not to let her past dictate her future after seeing what it had done to Junior.

Unlike his siblings, Junior was a ticking time bomb. Sheila always hoped he wouldn't hurt anyone, but figured it was only a matter of time before he did. Elizabeth and Claude tried everything to save their grandson from the demons that haunted him, but in the long run, he was a victim of circumstance.

CHAPTER TEN

A Family Reunion

BY THE END OF THE 70s, Junior was in jail for murder. Sheila had fallen in and out of love. She was living with her grandparents, going to school, and working a part-time job at New York Hospital, while raising two more children—this time her own. Darryl Jr. and Nicole were ages one and two. The Robinsons didn't mind Sheila staying there with her children, but she knew her grandparents were getting older and didn't want to be a burden on them. As luck would have it, an apartment would soon become available.

After a few years without contact, Evelyn reached out to the Robinsons—and found many things had changed. Sheila had a younger brother named TyRay and two children of her own, and all of them lived with the Robinsons. There was a vacancy in Evelyn's building, so she reached out to Pete McDougal, the property manager and a friend and business associate of Fritz, to secure the apartment for Sheila.

Sheila was only twenty-one, but what she'd been through made her mature enough to handle the responsibilities of living on her own and taking care of her own family. Sheila was excited to move into the same building because she'd sorely missed Evelyn and Richard. She longed for them all to be back together—she missed the laughter and fun they used to have before their father Clifford died.

Evelyn explained Sheila's situation to Pete McDougal and the building application was approved immediately. Richard had helped Mr. McDougal out of a few financial binds, so he was happy to do the favor. Elizabeth and Sheila went to J. Horn Furniture and purchased all the furniture for her new place the day after she moved into her fifth-floor, one-bedroom apartment with Darryl Jr., Nicole, and TyRay, who was now thirteen. Elizabeth was happy for Sheila and comfortable with her moving out, knowing Evelyn and Richard lived on the first floor.

While Sheila was settling into her new surroundings, unknown to her and Evelyn, Fritz was climbing up the ladder in the drug game. His name and reputation were ringing in the streets, because he was a good businessman and salesman and treated his customers with respect. Jealousy also became an issue because of the money he made and all the attention he got from the ladies. Richard's manhood would be challenged on numerous occasions by the dealers on the block.

Richard wasn't always known by the name Fritz. He went by his government name, Richard or Rich, until he saw the 1972 animated film, *Fritz the Cat*, based on a famous cartoon character in a sixties comic strip created by Robert Crumb. Fritz the Cat was a ladies' man, known for his smooth, self-assured, and easygoing personality, and his good deeds.[44] Fritz liked the name and thought he was a lot like the cat. It would soon become his street name and would stick with him throughout his time in the drug game.

44　　Fritz The Cat, Directed by Ralph Bakshi, Cinemation Industries, 1972. Film.

Fritz knew early on if he was going to be in the drug game, he had to be different. He needed to maintain respect and control the block, he had to fight for it, be fearless, ruthless, and be ready to die.

The dealers in the block found out quickly about the country boy whose clothes looked like hand-me-downs. The guy with the Jheri curls who stayed to himself and sat quietly on the stoop in front of 109. The one who fought as hard as he hustled to hold onto his. That was when Fritz gained their respect and several new friendships that would be instrumental in growing his drug enterprise.

The competing dealers across the street couldn't make any money after Fritz stole all their customers. Animosity was building all the time between the two groups. On the 4th of July tensions got high. It was a hot day when the guys across the street started shooting off huge, loud fireworks. Before long a bottle rocket made its way through the air and blew up not far from where Queen Bee and Fritz stood with his family, elders from the building, and neighborhood children playing outside 109.

Fritz marched across the street. "Y'all better watch them mutha fuckin' fireworks," he said.

The group of dealers surrounded Fritz.

"*No. No. No.* You better not touch him," Queen Bee demanded.

Fritz laughed. "Oh . . .y'all were gonna jump me?"

"Jump you? We were going to put your ass in the hospital," a guy named Rambo responded. He was called that because he liked to carry a huge survival knife like Rambo from the 1982 movie *First Blood*. Rambo liked to go on freebase binges, then use the knife to rob dust heads in the neighborhood.

That day, Queen Bee saved Fritz from getting the ultimate beat down. The dealers respected her and did whatever she asked because she looked out for them. Seeing how Fritz moved in the drug game and how he carried himself that day made allies out of enemies. Later, the group would work directly for Fritz.

When things got slow—if the block was too hot and they had to lay low from the cops, if there was bad weather or their drug supply was limited—Fritz and TJ would pass the time gambling in the hallway lobby, laughing, and listening to music on the boom box until a customer came by. There were nights friends came through to hang out with Fritz and TJ in front of the building. They would get too loud sometimes, forgetting they were outside Evelyn's window.

"Stop making all that fucking noise!" she would shout. "I got to go to work in the morning.

Evelyn's many warnings fell on death ears. One night Sheila, Fritz, TJ, and a few others were out late listening to music. Everyone was having a good time when Evelyn threw a bucket full of cold water out of the window. It missed them, hit the boom box, and that was the end of the concert.

Fritz didn't need music; he needed the money, which was why he worked long hours and late nights. He had big plans for his money. Hip-hop was steadily growing. Fritz wanted to branch into the entertainment industry, and buy real estate—he had recently looked at an abandoned factory building near the Hunts Point market in the Bronx. So Fritz worked, stacked, and saved.

"We gonna own the eighties," Fritz declared. "Everybody in Harlem is gonna owe me."

Fritz often said things that came true. By then TJ believed he could speak things into existence.

"I believe you," TJ responded.

It was great having the family back together again. It was like *All in the Family*.[45] Evelyn and Fritz were always coming upstairs and checking on Sheila and the children to make sure they had

---

[45] All In The Family, Created by Norman Lear, Johnny Speight, CBS, 1971-1979. TV Series.

what they needed. On Saturdays, Elizabeth would visit and take her granddaughter food shopping.

Everything was going well for a while. Sheila ran the house on a tight schedule. She would cook, clean, take care of the babies, and make sure TyRay got to school on time. Sheila's hectic work and school schedules made TyRay's behavior unmanageable at times. She needed Elizabeth to step in once in a while for reinforcement; she would get in that ass, and TyRay would straighten up for a minute. Then TyRay stopped going to school to hang with some young neighborhood thugs who were robbing people. He didn't work but would come home with a pocket full of money. Then he would turn the clock back, so Sheila didn't know what time he actually came in at night. Fritz, who was 21, eventually stepped in and took over, sitting TyRay down for a man-to-man talk.

"Stop the dumb shit and attracting so much attention to yourself. The more attention you draw, the more problems will follow. Instead of being a follower, think for yourself, and be your own man," Fritz told TyRay.

Fritz never had to threaten, holler, or scream at TyRay; when Fritz spoke, he listened, at least for a little while. It was 1979 and TyRay was 14 and mature for his age when Fritz suggested he move in with him on the sixth floor. There was no man in TyRay's life, and Fritz didn't want someone outside of family to be his role model. Fritz hoped to teach him what it was to be a black man, and teach him responsibility. Sheila wasn't worried about her younger brother—after all, he still came downstairs to have meals together. Fritz stayed at the apartment with TyRay from time to time, but was frequently absent. Fritz made his ultimatum clear: he would only pay rent if TyRay went to school and did what he was told.

While TyRay tried out independence, Sheila was dealing with her children's father. He was still in her life because of their children, coming by to visit them. He eased his way back into her heart with his sweet talk and Sheila was soon pregnant with their third child, Neil. Sheila gave him a second chance and quickly learned a zebra never changes his stripes, and a cheat would always be a cheat.

TyRay was a big help at home while Sheila was pregnant with Neil. The talk with Fritz and living on his own did TyRay a lot of good; he changed for the better. He matured quickly, graduated junior high school, and helped Sheila out with the babies when she needed him. The more reliable TyRay became, the more responsibilities Fritz entrusted in him. In turn, Fritz would often give him spending money and even bought him a car.

Fritz was always generous, especially when it came to family and friends. Fritz spent money as fast as he got it because it came to him so easily. He was blessed like that. While Fritz was selling and stacking his money made with Queen Bee, he also reaped rewards at the crap tables and playing numbers. Gambling was a way of life in Harlem, an easy way to make a quick buck and lots of money if you were lucky or good at it. Fritz was both.

Fritz started out playing the bolita (a type of lottery popular in Cuba and among Florida's working-class Hispanic, Italian, and black populations). In the basic bolita game, 100 small balls are placed into a bag and mixed thoroughly, and bets are taken on which number will be drawn. Fritz would bet $1.50 on two numbers and win $150.[46] After hitting the bolita numerous times he would play all three numbers straight, meaning much more money in his pockets. Just like that he was on a winning streak, hitting numbers back-to-back. He liked the odds and his chances.

---

46   Wikipedia contributors, "Bolita," Wikipedia, The Free Encyclopedia, https://en.wikipedia.org/w/index.php?title=Bolita&oldid=915552578 (accessed December 3, 2019).

Fritz was so confident about his game that he once bet Evelyn's bill money on a number.

Evelyn gave Fritz money to pay rent and electricity, and he made a detour to the number spot down the hall. A few days later, Evelyn realized the rent wasn't paid, and when the lights went off, she put two and two together. She couldn't hold back her anger. She scolded Fritz like he was a child.

"You ain't pay the bills? I'm going to bust that ass," Evelyn yelled. "I got this," Fritz promised.

"When I come home from work you better have my lights on."

Evelyn came home that evening and the lights were on; Fritz had hit the number for 10 Gs ($10,000). Fritz put the rent in Evelyn's hand, sent her to Atlantic City, and gave Sheila and TyRay pocket money.

Sheila was high on life. She was on an exhilarating roller coaster ride, with no baby daddy and not a care in the world. She was independent, her children were healthy, and Fritz made sure she was never in need of money.

The older folks in the neighborhood loved Fritz because he took care of them, gave money for groceries and rent, money for their children's back-to-school clothes, threw block parties and cookouts, and sponsored bus rides out of the city. Fritz was a southern boy, raised to take care of and respect his elders. They made Fritz a part of their entourage, and he considered them a part of his extended family. On warm mornings, the older neighbors sat on the stoop drinking coffee and reading Big Red. This was a cheaply printed, daily publication sold at newsstands, offering tips and tactics for landing the next big winning number. Older men and women held the newest Big Red in their hands waiting for Fritz, so lucky with his betting. Like clockwork, he'd join the old folks on the stoop, give them a tip, and soon they were hitting the number too.

Fritz played his numbers like clockwork. If he couldn't get to the number spot, he'd send someone. There was a meat market on 113th Street that was also a number spot, operated and owned by the Mafia.

Fritz once sent his childhood friend, Danny, to put down a bet of $1,000.

"You putting that much on a number? I need to know what you know," the customer at the meat market said when Danny placed his bet.

"I've seen a guy come in here in dirty sneakers and jeans and put more than that on numbers," another customer said. Danny knew the customer was talking about Fritz, but he just smiled, played the number, and left.

Did Fritz hit that day? Maybe. Fritz played numbers and hit all the time. One time he hit so big, the bookie asked to see him later, as he didn't have enough money to pay out. Fritz got his money, but now the word was out. Harlem bookies refused to take Fritz's bets because the large payouts would hurt their business. So Fritz switched it up, had family place smaller bets for him. He gave Claude a number and the number came out. Claude didn't know he hit until Fritz told him. The bookie came by the house the next day with a big-ass suitcase full of money for Claude. Sheila was there visiting her grandparents and looked at them all, amazed. She couldn't believe her eyes: the suitcase held stacks of large crisp bills wrapped in bundles with bank currency bands.

Either Fritz had the Big Red down to a science or he was just clairvoyant. He knew what numbers didn't play and played in a calendar year, and what numbers didn't play this week and the week before. Some people compared Fritz to Russell Crowe's character in *A Beautiful Mind*.[47] He was a mathematical genius, so

---

[47] A Beautiful Mind, Directed by Ron Howard, Imagine Entertainment, 2001. Film.

good with numbers he could've been a successful accountant if he had gone to college. Knowing how to pick and win numbers came to him easily. He had the Midas touch—everything he touched turned into gold.

Fritz eventually moved from the numbers game to the craps tables.

He would gamble away tens of thousands of dollars in the crap spots: Joe Grant (111th and St. Nicholas), the S & S (145th and 8th), and the Zodiac (145th and Bradhurst). He'd gamble all day and all night, sometimes for days, running out of money, sending a guy to his house to bring him more. He didn't even get upset about losing. Some people thought Fritz was out of control or would go broke because of cash he threw away at the craps table. But he was never that reckless. He knew his limits and had the extra cash put to the side for a pastime he enjoyed.

Unfortunately, life wasn't all about the highs. And people were rarely prepared for the lows.

CHAPTER ELEVEN

Death's Toll

July 29, 1979 was a beautiful, cool Sunday morning. Sheila, now six months pregnant, asked TyRay to babysit Darryl Jr. and Nicole. She then left for the laundromat with Evelyn's help. When they returned, there were an unusual amount of people gathered on the block. It was such a nice day, they didn't think it was odd.

Sheila sat on the stoop to catch her breath while Evelyn dropped off laundry at her apartment. When Sheila entered her apartment a few minutes later, she found Nicole standing quietly in the middle of her bedroom and Darryl Jr. lying on the bed with TyRay, who seemed to be in a catatonic state. He kept his eyes on the baby but was unable to speak. Darryl Jr. seemed okay, but something in the air felt wrong. The next words Sheila heard chilled her.

"Baby fall out the window," Nicole said.

What? Confused, Sheila looked at the open window and saw that her flower boxes were gone, then saw them shattered and spread across the alley below. She ran out of the apartment in shock, rushing downstairs in a panic to get Evelyn, and instead found Fritz in the lobby. She was shaking as she told him what happened. Fritz was convinced she'd heard wrong, and came back upstairs with Sheila.

It was clear something was wrong. The room was too quiet. Fritz walked over to Darryl Jr., who was still and unmoving on the bed. The baby didn't respond as he lay in Fritz's arms.

TyRay finally spoke among his sister's cries and disbelief. "I didn't want you to see him like that…in the alley," TyRay whispered. He dropped his head, unable to face them.

"I went downstairs…" he continued slowly. "I picked him up. I didn't want you to see him," TyRay repeated.

At that point, Fritz was already out of the apartment with the baby in his arms and Sheila behind him with Nicole in hers. Someone had called the cops and they were outside when the family ran to them. Seeing the officers, Fritz headed back upstairs to check on TyRay, who was not doing well. Then the family—Sheila, Fritz, Evelyn, and the Robinsons—rushed to the St. Luke's Hospital on Amsterdam Avenue.

They waited in the ER for the doctor's update on Darryl Jr.'s condition. The doctors came out and Sheila hurried to meet them. There was a mother's heart-wrenching scream that echoed through the hospital, followed by silence, as doctors informed Sheila that her son had sustained severe internal injuries and did not survive. She'd just seen him. He was just in her arms. But he was now gone.

Sheila wouldn't speak again for many days after. But what the family thought was normal grieving was something else. She eventually tried to speak but couldn't. She pointed to her throat in panic when she couldn't hear her own voice. She was diagnosed with Selective Mutism (SM), an anxiety disorder in which a person who is normally capable of speech cannot speak in specific situations or to specific people. Doctors said her voice would return with counseling and time.

A couple of days later, Sheila was on her way home when she was stopped in the street by a reporter and a news crew who came to investigate the incident. A reporter shocked her by accusing TyRay of pushing the baby out of the window. She threatened them with a lawsuit if they printed that lie.[48] TyRay had already been through enough.

TyRay loved his nephew and niece. He'd never hurt them. It was an accident, and everyone knew that. While Sheila was out doing laundry with Evelyn, TyRay was left to babysit the children. He had bathed and dressed Nicole as requested, then bathed Darryl Jr. He wanted to help Sheila as much as he could during her pregnancy. He had left the children alone only for a few minutes to tidy up the kitchen before Sheila came home. There were no window guards in households with children back then; it was a different time. TyRay, traumatized and in shock, saw that his nephew had fallen five stories. In a daze he'd run downstairs, retrieved Darryl Jr.'s frail, battered body from the alley, and placed him on the bed as if asleep. Then he'd sat there, speechless, until confronted by Fritz. It was all unimaginable.

Elizabeth made the funeral arrangements. Darryl Jr.'s father was unable to attend the funeral, having been stabbed a few days before. He was fighting for his life in the ICU when his son was buried.

Darryl Jr.'s funeral was held at St. Luke A.M.E. Church on Amsterdam Ave and 153rd Street. It was well attended by family, friends, neighbors, and many people from the community, who lined up to give their support, prayers, and condolences. Their brother Junior— still in prison—had a temporary pass to attend

---

48   Boy, 1, Falls 5 Floors to Death." The New York Times Archives, 30 July 1979, Section B, Page 2, https://www.nytimes.com/1979/07/30/archives/boy-1-falls-5-floors-to-death.html.

his nephew's funeral. It was the first time he had ever seen Darryl Jr. in person. When Junior walked up and saw his baby nephew in the tiny casket, he lost it. He broke down and cried uncontrollably. The CO who had accompanied him tried to comfort him, but Junior was overcome with grief. They helped Junior outside for some fresh air and made the decision to take him back to prison early. Sheila cried as she gave Junior a hug and then watched him leave.

Sheila was on the funeral program to speak a few words on her son's behalf, but it was still difficult to get complete sentences out. At the podium, she could no longer hold it together. Instead, she put her head down and cried. She prayed to God as she cried. Eventually Elizabeth steered her to her seat, where she sobbed in her arms.

Evelyn took care of Nicole and TyRay, while Sheila stayed with her grandparents. For weeks, Sheila carried a pad and a pen everywhere to help her communicate, and couldn't leave the house without a chaperone. Every day she tried to speak. Sheila's brain was working fine, she knew what she wanted to say, but the words were stuck in her throat. Every day she grew more impatient and frustrated. Eventually Sheila returned to the apartment on 112th Street. Fritz and Evelyn had promised to stop by every day. Fritz had everyone in the building and block under strict orders: Don't bring up the baby.

At night, the apartment was eerily quiet, a too-quiet that made Sheila uncomfortable. She was used to being surrounded by her children with their special laughter and noise. She had insomnia, and when she did try to sleep, she would hear a baby crying. She'd climb out of bed and walk through the apartment, searching for a baby she could never find.

Mostly Sheila would lie in bed wide awake, thinking she must be having a nervous breakdown. Eventually she looked for ways to occupy her time—she would rearrange the furniture or clean the entire apartment from top to bottom. 'Being heavily pregnant didn't stop her.

Sheila delivered Neil full-term on October 23, 1979, three months after Darryl Jr.'s death. She didn't dare pick up or touch Neil for days after he was born, because he looked so much like Darryl Jr. it scared her. Fritz, Evelyn, and TyRay stepped in to care for Neil.

A few days later, after a trip to see her doctor Sheila stopped by Evelyn's house to visit with her kids. It had been several months since Darryl Jr.'s death and Sheila was still not able to speak complete sentences.

"Sheila, I don't know when you're going to be able to talk, but I'm sure your kids would want to hear you say something," Evelyn said.

Sheila then wrote on her pad: *I'm working at that.*

"I would love you to say something. I want you to respond to me. I want you to stop writing on that paper. I want to hear your voice."

Sheila wanted to talk. If Evelyn only knew how frustrated she was and how hard it was for her that she couldn't. Sheila felt that no one could really understand, not even her therapist, who she had stopped seeing. Frustrated, she left Evelyn's house and returned home.

Sheila was tired and went to bed early. She was awakened by the sounds of a baby crying, and knew it wasn't Neil, because Neil and Nicole were with Evelyn. It became clear that Sheila must have dreamt it. She closed her eyes and almost drifted back to sleep when she heard a baby crying again, but this time she felt something touched her. Sheila jumped out of bed screaming, and her heart racing. She felt a chill cover her body and seep down to her bones. Then she opened her mouth and spoke clear and complete sentences: "Are you here, baby? I know you're here, Darryl. I know you want to help me."

Sheila couldn't believe she was speaking. The fear that gripped her when she woke was completely gone. Sheila hurried to the bathroom, looked in the mirror, and slowly opened her lips, saying her name. Sheila!

She got dressed fast and hurried downstairs to Evelyn's apartment.

She needed Evelyn to hear her speak.

Evelyn opened the door. "I'm cooking, want some dinner?" she asked.

"Yes, I do," Sheila said.

"What? You're talking?" Evelyn yelled, then she pulled Sheila inside and over to the phone. She called Sheila's grandmother and then anybody else she could think of to give them the news. A few minutes later Fritz walked in with Neil and started to change his diaper. It was a trying time for Fritz. He loved being there for his family, but it was a lot taking care of Sheila's kids, looking after her too, while making sure he was on top of his drug business. At times the stress showed on Fritz's face. Every day he wished Sheila would get better.

"Do you want me to do that?" Sheila asked with a big grin.

Fritz looked at her and laughed. "Well it's about time. I knew you'd get your voice back. It was just a matter of time," he said, then gave Sheila a big hug. Fritz was finally able to explain how stressed he was by her silence and depression. It made him feel weak and helpless — he was the problem solver who couldn't solve Sheila's condition.

Sheila began to cry. Then they all laughed and after that, became closer than ever. None could guess that tragedy would strike again.

Queen Bee didn't always do right by her workers, which also benefited Fritz when dealers switched sides and came to work for him.

Queen Bee had habits, like getting high on her own supply. Every time you saw her, she was sniffing. She had no shame in her game. She'd be in the hallway of 109—pulling out a piece of aluminum foil or a small Ziploc bag of coke and a straw from her purse, sniffing and not caring who saw. She'd then take the same piece of aluminum foil or Ziploc and sell it to a customer. This habit of indulging during work hours and diluting the quality of the product made it weak and harder to sell. It was an issue for the customer coming to buy and the workers trying to get rid of the product. Paying workers on time or even at all also became a problem.

"Shit is tight," Queen Bee would say. "I need y'all to sell this product. I'll hit y'all off with a few dollars right now and make it up to you on the next package." In an illegal economy, there weren't many people who could do what she was doing and get away with it.

Meanwhile, she'd give workers packages she knew were trash because of all the cutting. She'd dilute the coke using baking soda or some other substance, mixing four grams of coke with one or more grams of baking soda and have the workers sell it as five grams. Customers were complaining and the worker would bring the product back to Queen Bee, who'd convince him he wasn't hustling right. The truth was, Queen Bee was getting old—she was in her early sixties— and didn't want to go back to jail. She didn't have the same drive as she did back in the day. Her health was not the best and she'd put on excessive amounts of weight over the years.

Besides, times were changing quickly. The quality of street heroin wasn't the same after the French Connection bust, which had been providing the vast majority of heroin used in the United States, and street hustling was for the young. Queen Bee had watched Fritz grow from peddling clothes to helping TJ almost quadruple her drug business. She knew Fritz was ambitious, had the potential to be a good boss, and most strikingly, had outgrown her. She was good with the few dollars she made off the drugs she sold and could maintain her lifestyle, but she could no longer provide Fritz with the quantity he needed to sustain his own business. The connect Queen Bee had wasn't reliable anymore either; Fritz sold out faster than the connect could reup. It was a huge problem for Fritz, who refused to lose customers over that.

In the summer of 1979, Queen Bee located another heroin source, an older gentleman called Dopeman. Dopeman was from uptown and hung out in Renny's Bar & Lounge on 138th and 7th. Queen Bee then made the important introductions. Dopeman gave Fritz a few ounces of heroin on consignment, and Fritz put the heroin on the streets immediately. Less than three days later, Dopeman sent two guys down to 112th Street to collect his money.

Fritz bargained with Dopeman's collection guys for more time while dealing with more problems: Dopeman's drugs were inferior and Fritz's drug fiend customers turned elsewhere. Rumors swirled that Dopeman had given him a suicide package of bad drugs, knowing Fritz would be stuck with bad product and in debt to him.

A few days had passed, and Fritz was still having a difficult time selling the dope. Fritz went uptown to talk with Dopeman.

"The dope's not selling," Fritz said.

"That's your problem, not mine," Dopeman responded. "I need time."

"Business is business, and I need my money sooner than later," Dopeman replied.

"And once I pay you . . . our business is done," Fritz said before leaving.

Fritz knew that in the drug game very few played fair and danger was always lurking around the corner, but wasn't prepared when it came knocking at his door.

Fritz had gone upstairs to Sheila's house to hang out like he did every day. They chatted, laughed, and he spent time with his niece and nephew. It was a typical, pleasant evening and the family was supposed to be going out to eat. Sheila was tired, and decided to stay in and cook. Fritz went downstairs and planned to return later to eat.

Fritz headed over to 112th Street and St. Nicholas and ran into one of his dealers, who was having problems selling Dopeman's supply. "This is what it is, until things change!" Fritz told him.

TJ was heading over and overheard this argument. He thought little of it—Fritz had to put people in line, part of the job—and told him he'd come back with a tuna sandwich for him.

A few minutes later. TJ heard shots outside his apartment window, and Sheila was startled by a sudden pounding on the door. It was a frantic neighbor.

"Your brother just got shot!" the older woman shouted.

Sheila couldn't believe what she was hearing, because she'd just seen him. *How?* She thought.

"I need you to watch the children," Sheila said to her neighbor.

Then she grabbed a coat and ran out.

When she got downstairs the first thing she saw was TJ leaning over Fritz, who lay in a pool of blood. Rambo and some other guys from the block circled them protectively. Fritz was still alert and trying to speak. Someone pulled a car around and they rushed him to Harlem Hospital.

The hospital was packed with well-wishers and those seeking revenge. Word on the street was that Fritz had been shot several times by two of Dopeman's henchmen in front of Martin's Game Room (now D's Girl's Hair Studio). It was a spot frequented by neighborhood dealers and children, who played arcade games there for hours.

Fritz spent hours in surgery. Five bullets were removed from his body, and he needed several blood transfusions to save his life.

Fritz was in intensive care for weeks before he finally showed signs of improvement. When Fritz was strong enough to be moved, he was taken to his mother's house in Charleston, South Carolina, to recuperate.

1980s

RICHARD ALLEN SIMMONS
112th Street "Fritz"

CHAPTER TWELVE

Rise of the King Of Kingpins

THE ROAD TO RECOVERY WAS tough for Fritz. Lying around not making money added to his frustration. Since he was unable to do much else, Fritz became an avid news watcher. The wheels started spinning in his head when he saw a news report about the crack epidemic. He listened intently to news about the Colombian cartel war to control various territories in major US cities, including New York, Miami, San Francisco, Houston, and Chicago.[49] Before getting shot, Fritz had established a relationship with an associate of the Medellín Cartel, and now he looked forward to rekindling it when he got back to Harlem.

---

49 Wikipedia contributors, "Illegal drug trade in Colombia," Wikipedia, The Free Encyclopedia, https://en.wikipedia.org/w/index.php?title=Illegal_drug_trade_in_Colombia&ol did=928839902 (accessed December 3, 2019).

Fritz returned to 112th Street two years later, strong mentally and physically. He was focused on exacting revenge on Dopeman, who ordered his hit, and the men who carried it out. No one thought it was a coincidence that the people involved were systematically killed. Very few people ever knew the truth, and criminal investigations proved too little to press charges.

Prior to any of that, Fritz was determined to pick up where he left off in the drug game. But now he needed to gather trusted soldiers and generate extra capital after being away for so long. Fritz had left a bit of money in his personal stash, a secret safe installed in his apartment at 109. Fritz set about playing numbers and frequenting the crap tables at Joe Grant, the S & S, and the Zodiac. Fritz normally saved the money he made hustling and had a good reputation in the streets, so it wasn't hard for him to get back up. Fritz eventually linked up with his Medellín connect, whom he'd met while selling heroin for Queen Bee.

Fritz then arranged for TJ to meet him near 111th Street. He had an urgent matter he needed to discuss, away from the block, away from prying eyes and big ears. He took TJ for a walk along Central Park North.

"We getting ready to get paid," Fritz said. "What you mean?" TJ asked.

"I just got 15 keys of coke on consignment." "Fifteen?" TJ repeated. He couldn't believe it. "And I'ma give it away on consignment."

TJ was speechless. Consignment was risky. What if his people ran off with the coke and left him owing?

Fritz promised he knew what he was doing. "I know just who to give it to. Don't worry, we gonna be good."

In the '80s cocaine was everywhere, and a fortune could be made with the right connection. The Medellín Cartel was a highly organized network of drug suppliers and smugglers from the city of Medellín, Colombia. The cartel operated from the 1970s into the early 1990s.[50] It was considered the richest and most ruthless drug-trafficking organization in the world, and one of its founders, Pablo Emilio Escobar Gaviria, was the most powerful, violent, and feared criminal in history. The cartel smuggled tons of cocaine into countries all over the world each week and brought in between $60–$70m *daily* in drug profits, making an estimated $22–$26b a year. Twenty-six billion.

The Cali Cartel was based in southern Colombia, surrounding the city of Cali and the Valle del Cauca. Its founders were the Rodríguez Orejuela brothers and José Santacruz Londoño.[51] First they trafficked marijuana, but soon shifted their focus to cocaine, a more lucrative drug. In the early 1970s the Cali Cartel set up a distribution center in New York City.

During the '70s the DEA was more concerned about cracking down on heroin. It was thought to be more problematic because of the rise in crime, the many Vietnam vets coming home strung out, and the high overdose rate.

The Medellín and Cali cartels divided up the four major United States distribution points, with Cali taking New York City and the Medellín taking Florida and Miami. That left Los Angeles as a free-for-all. The war between these two cartels in the mid-1980s brought in large quantities of cocaine pouring

---

50 Wikipedia contributors, "Medellín Cartel," Wikipedia, The Free Encyclopedia, https://en.wikipedia.org/w/index.php?title=Medell%C3%ADn_Cartel&oldid=925736530 (acce ssed December 3, 2019).

51 Wikipedia contributors, "Cali Cartel," Wikipedia, The Free Encyclopedia, https://en.wikipedia.org/w/index. php?title=Cali_Cartel&oldid=928020899 (accessed December 3, 2019).

into the United States that needed to be unloaded quickly. The cartels lowered their prices or gave it away on consignment. The war became a street dealer's dream come true, and for many, a rag-to-riches story. This historic excess of cocaine helped Fritz grow his drug empire quickly.

Through the Medellín Cartel, he received 15 kilos (keys) of cocaine on consignment, and was set to make $6,000 a key—$90,000 if he could sell it in a week. Fritz knew he could: word of mouth was powerful, and his product was consistently good. He sold all the coke in two weeks, immediately reestablishing his long-term business relationship with his connect.

Fritz soon became Harlem's biggest cocaine dealer, employing hundreds of men and women throughout the five boroughs and neighboring cities including Philly, DC, and Baltimore. He earned the title King of Consignment among customers and dealers alike. He distributed kilos on a kingpin level, selling to many well-known heavy hitters in Harlem like Rich Porter, Allen Lord, and Spanish Miguel.

Dealers from Hamilton Heights, Manhattanville, Sugar Hill, Spanish Harlem, Washington Heights, and the surrounding boroughs all bought from Fritz.

In Harlem, Fritz's name was ringing out as loudly as Catholic church bells. Those in his inner circle began calling Fritz "Nicholai," after the widely used Russian name that meant "victory of the people." Others called him Nick, a nod to the infamous Nicky Barnes of St. Nicholas Avenue and 112th.

Leroy "Nicky" Barnes was a crime boss in the 1970s, labeled Mister Untouchable by the *New York Times*. In 1981, however, Barnes offered to cooperate with federal authorities after they showed him proof that his close drug partner had been cheating him, sleeping with both his wife and his girlfriend, and doing drugs in front of his two young daughters.[52] Barnes was eventually labeled a rat and snitch, losing his kingpin status and his street creditability, which opened the door for the rise of Nicholai.

Fritz's empire clashed with a severe economic recession affecting much of the developed world in the late 1970s and early 1980s. When unemployment was at an all-time high, people knew they could work for Fritz or one of his elicit businesses to feed their families. He knew how to survive the streets, think outside of the box, and move strategically. Another major strength was his charisma: he could get almost anyone, man or woman, to do as he commanded.

Fritz's office was on 112th Street, and his employees were the residents who occupied the six-story apartment building. Fritz made sure their families were straight financially: their rent and tuitions paid, their children clothed and fed, and ample food at the dinner tables. They weren't just neighbors, but Fritz's extended family. They loved Fritz and would do anything to protect him.

One day, Big Gee, an associate of Fritz, came looking for Chucky.

Big Gee helped with the dogs at The Pit, the dog fighting ring Fritz ran with his best friend, Chucky. Chucky was Fritz's friend and brother, but he was also The Enforcer. He lived in 109 with his family— his common-law wife, Shelagh, and their three children.

---

52   Burnstein, Scott. "The Love Triangle That Killed "The Council": How Romance & Betrayal Buried Historic Harlem Kingpin Consortium." The Gangster Report, https:// gangsterreport.com/the-love-triangle-that-killed-the-council-how-romance-betrayal-buried-historic-harlem-kingpin-consortium/ (accessed December 3, 2019).

"Yo Chucky. Yo Chucky," Big Gee called out, hoping Chucky would look out a window and see him outside. No one responded.

Big Gee questioned the elderly women sitting on the stoop of 109. They pretended not to hear him. When pressed, one woman, Ms. Mae, looked at Big Gee across, up, and down, then finally answered, "No we ain't seen no Chucky."

Big Gee walked to Martin's Game Room, which Chucky managed. He wasn't there either. He returned to the women on the stoop. "I know you ain't seen Chucky, but did you see Fritz?" Big Gee now asked.

Ms. Mae and the other woman stood, entered the building, and returned concealing something in their hands as they sat back down. Big Gee assumed they went to get Fritz, but then two more older women got up and did the same thing. *What the hell is going on?* Big Gee thought. He finally walked away, only to hear someone saying clearly: "Big boy lookin' for you," Ms. Mae said loudly.

"Oh, that's my brother," Chucky said. Big Gee turned in surprise. "We don't know him," one of the women said firmly. Chucky introduced Big Gee to each of them.

Ms. Mae said, "Now we know you." She then turned to the other women. "Put them cups back." She directed calmly. The women had secretly filled cups with a lye solution (lye-cups). If Big Gee had threatened them or one of their people, the lye-cups would've hit Big Gee in the face, turning it into what the Mexican-American drug cartel assassins called *pozole*, a traditional Mexican stew.

Love for Fritz and Chucky on 112th was endless.

Queen Bee was instrumental in teaching Fritz the game, and the student soon surpassed the teacher. Fritz was good with people, especially the ladies, who were more trustworthy than the men and who helped grow his business. Gwen and Peggy were friends of Fritz, but also knew the streets and the hustlers. They were instrumental in helping build Fritz's business.

Gwen had chestnut colored skin, with a warm brown finish. She was attractive, shapely and had a smile that was contagious and lit up a room—she was a people person. She was also a mover and shaker. She frequented the after-hours and gambling spots, and they knew her by name. Gwen knew everyone: the gamblers, the hustlers, and the women who dated them. She mixed with a variety of people and made a lot of money with Fritz. Gwen had the clientele and Fritz had the drugs, at the right price. She was completely loyal to Fritz and he relied on her to help move his drugs. Their relationship was the perfect match in the drug world.

Peggy was big, built, and boisterous. She could go toe-to-toe with any man in a boxing ring and hold her own. Peggy was Fritz's personal assistant, a girl Friday, and a good friend. Peggy ran errands, did the laundry, cut and bagged the drugs. She cleaned the apartment often and thoroughly from top to bottom. The problem with Peggy, however, was that she loved coke. There were times when Fritz would leave Peggy alone with a tray piled high with coke on the table. Peggy wouldn't touch it, but when Fritz came back Peggy would ask, "Yo, I know you gonna give me some of that, right?"

Peggy lived across the street from Fritz. Her building was a known shooting gallery, and almost every other apartment was used for that purpose. Riverboat, Peggy's neighbor, had the apartment where most people went to shoot heroin. I assume he adopted the name, since he was a country boy from Mississippi and the first River Boat was introduced on the Mississippi River. Riverboat charged people to use his place. His shooting gallery had everything you needed to get high, and the best dope on the westside of Harlem. Back then if you went into a shooting gallery you could purchase the setup, everything you needed to get high—the dope and the needle. If you didn't have money to buy the setup, you used someone else's needle if they were finished and wanted to give it to you. Fritz often used Riverboat's apartment to test out the quality of his heroin, using Peggy as a courier. It was convenient as she lived in the same building. Fifteen St. Nicholas Avenue became Fritz's dope spot.

It was all business with these women; sex was a distraction and not part of the equation. This was important, as he had seen many men before him lose it all over sex. Nicky Barnes was a prime example of this.

In the mid-80s, Fritz had made enough money playing the numbers and selling drugs to open up a nightclub. It was something he'd always wanted to do, own a legitimate business and invest in real estate. In 1985 Fritz opened the Uptown Garage on West 127th Street and Convent and put Gwen in charge as the club manager. It's now an abandoned, boarded-up building, but back then it was one of the hottest party spots in Harlem. It had four stories, a lower-level parking lot, two dance floors with a bar and deejay booth, and a penthouse where the high rollers gambled. On opening night at least 1,500 people showed up, and lines to get in usually wrapped around the corner. Many nights it would be packed to capacity.

BMWs and Mercedes lined the curb. Some of them had Gucci, Louis Vuitton, Fendi, and MCM interiors custom-de-signed by Harlem's Dapper Dan. Dan is a famous African-American fashion designer from Harlem. Dapper Dan's Boutique operated from 1982 to 1992, and was most associated with introducing high fashion to the hip-hop world.[53]

---

[53] Safronova, Valeriya. "Inside Dapper Dan and Gucci's Harlem Atelier." The New York Times, Fashion, 20 March 2018, https://www.nytimes.com/2018/03/20/fashion/gucci-dapper-dan-atelier-harlem.html.

The young ballers who pulled up in the fancy cars were always blinged out in diamonds and gold jewelry. Their Gianni Versace suits were tailored, the gators on their feet were spit-shined, and mink coats were worn with matching fur hats.

The ladies wore sequined dresses and all type of furs: short, three-quarter, or even floor length. Their hair was immaculate, their makeup flawless, their fingers and toes freshly painted. This was to be expected from a young lady seeking a baller, and they were sure to find them at the Uptown Garage.

A year after the club opened, Fritz threw Sheila a birthday party in the VIP Section. Fritz loved showing people a good time on their birthday and took it to the extreme. There was the clowning and playing around that Fritz started, which became a birthday ritual on 112th Street. Fritz always got two cakes for birthdays—one to eat and one to wear.

It was Fritz's 25th birthday, October 8th, 1982, and he was all dressed up for the occasion. His friends had vowed to get him back for his birthday antics. They gathered at his apartment for a small celebration and when Fritz went to blow out the candles, they pushed his face into it. Fritz laughed it off, but he didn't forget.

Sheila's birthday followed a few months later in January. She was dressed to the nines, hair done, and rocking a full-length mink. She had just come in from celebrating a fabulous evening with Arnold Cooley, the father of her fourth child, Raven. The lights were out in 109 and the elevator was not working. The elevator did break down from time to time, but there hadn't been a major city blackout since 1977. This blackout only seemed to be in her building.

Arnold helped Sheila up the stairs to the fifth floor. When she went to put her key in, the door opened on its own.

"*Surprise!*" Fritz yelled, then he hit Sheila directly in the face with a cake.

The apartment was filled with family, friends, and neighbors. There was plenty of food and bottles of Dom Pérignon. Fritz had gone all out with this elaborate birthday surprise, involving the entire building. It was a nice gesture, but he'd also done it to be mean, and Sheila was very upset. Cake was in her hair and chunks of it was stuck to the front of her mink coat. Fritz couldn't stop laughing.

"Happy birthday," Fritz chuckled.

"Happy birthday my ass!" Sheila said, showing him the damage to her fur.

"So what?" Fritz said, then pulled a thick stack of money from his pocket and slapped it into Sheila's hand. "Now go buy you another coat and get your hair done."

By the end of the night the party turned into a full-on neighborhood food fight. It wasn't always all business. 112th Street knew how to have fun. If you lived on the block and Fritz knew it was your birthday, there was no place to hide: You were going to be wearing your birthday cake by the end of the night.

Sheila was excited about celebrating her 30th birthday at the Uptown Garage. When she got to the club that night, Fritz surprised her at the door—with two double magnum-sized champagne bottles.

"Now go and enjoy your birthday," he laughed, ushering Sheila inside.

This was the first time Sheila celebrated her birthday in the club, and she didn't have a good time… she had a *great* time, dancing and drinking with friends. The bartender almost spoiled that night.

Sheila's friends were drinking a lot more than she was, so when she tried to get another bottle the bartender refused to accommodate her. Fritz had to let all the bartenders know, *This my sister and whatever she wants, y'all give it to her, I got that.* Fritz always paid the tab for family when they dropped by and made sure the register was right at the end of the night. Sheila continued to enjoy her evening, floating through the club checking out the scenery. She was amazed and proud of what Fritz was able to do with the space. She was impressed with all the people that had come out to show him love. At the end of the night she went searching through the crowd to say goodbye to her brother and wound up in the penthouse, where the guys played c-low, craps, poker, and blackjack.

There were a few women but a lot more men around the game tables. There were thousands of dollars being gambled. Sheila was feeling lucky and knew how to play c-low: It was a dice game, played with three dice, where the highest roll wins, 4-5-6 takes all, and 6-6-6 is the highest roll. Sheila used to play dice with her brothers and their friends in the hallway at night, always getting her little change up, and then she'd leave. She knew when to cut her losses. She would remind herself that she didn't want a nigga walking away with her winnings.

Sheila stood around and watched the guys gambling for a while. After she made up her mind, she put down her bet at the c-low table, picked up the dice, and rolled. She started out her bet with $150 and stopped playing after she reached $3,000. She then picked up her winnings and turned to leave.

"You can't do that," a guy at the table said.

When you gamble in illegal spots, it can get ugly. Some guys don't like losing or playing with people looking for a quick come-up, not investing time or big money in the game. He clearly didn't know that Sheila was Fritz's sister—she wasn't at the club often, after all. Someone told him, and he quickly and effusively apologized. Then Sheila left the club with a magnum of champagne and a few more dollars in her handbag.

The Uptown Garage was open for about two years until the

cops started coming around. They were looking to shut it down because of the gambling and occasional drug sales. Fritz had much to lose and at the time was already grossing hundreds of thousands of dollars a week on the streets of Harlem, so instead of keeping the club open and attracting unnecessary attention, Fritz shut the spot down six months later.

Fritz was known to recruit family into the business. TyRay was 20 years old, living upstairs with Fritz, and had been exposed to a lot of criminal activity. Fritz thought that TyRay would rather hustle for his own money than rob and stick up people, which he was currently doing. Fritz also thought that at 20, he was ready. TyRay, though, was like his brother Junior—neither liked to listen, and both were given many opportunities they managed to mess up.

In the summer of 1986 Sheila was arrested and spent a day at Rikers Island that felt like a lifetime. It started out as a beautiful, sunny day. She was living in Yonkers and recently gave birth to Howard, her fifth child, when TyRay came to visit. She had gained a lot of weight after having the baby and wasn't feeling her usual confidence. TyRay gave her money for her and the kids to go on a shopping spree. At the time she jokingly thought, *Damn, I must be going to jail… TyRay is cheap and don't give nobody money.* After shopping, she put on one of her new outfits and they all went to 112th Street to see her family.

Sheila brought the baby over to meet his Uncle Fritz. Nothing had changed since she left 109. There were the usual guys from the building and around the way, hanging out in the hallways playing dice. Sheila went to lie down with the baby on Fritz's bed. She was having physical discomfort postpartum and taking it easy. There was nothing strange about the day until TyRay ran in, grabbed two bags filled with money Fritz had stacked in the corner, and left.

Instead of leaving immediately to be where he needed to be, he decided to stop and play C-low with the guys in the hallway. TyRay, like some of his other siblings, was a gambler at heart. Fritz and Sheila were in the apartment laughing and talking. Suddenly they heard the loud buzz of police walkie-talkies and commotion in the hallway. They looked out the window and saw the familiar bright lights of cop cars outside the building.

They would later find out that police were in the building responding to a domestic abuse call, a call about a man allegedly carrying a shotgun. It turned out to be a classic wrong place, wrong time scenario. Or for TyRay, at least. When the cops frisked the guys in the hallway playing dice, there was TyRay, with the bags of money next to him.

The cop in charge let everyone go except TyRay, "The guy with all the money."

Now neighbors were gathering in front of 109. Sheila handed Howard to his godmother Jackie through the window. Then she turned to Fritz.

"Open the door so I can go out to see what's going on, and close it quickly behind me," she told him.

Fritz opened the door just wide enough for her to squeeze through, but a white cop was standing at the door with his gun in her face.

"You know I can blow your fucking head off right!" the cop screamed. "Tell that person to open the fucking door!"

"No, I'm not going to tell my brother to open the door," Sheila said, standing with her back to the door. "It's never going to be on my conscience that I was the cause of you killing my brother."

The cop pulled out his handcuffs and immediately arrested Sheila along with TyRay, who was already handcuffed in the hallway.

Another cop was banging on Fritz's door while two others stood ready with their guns already out the holsters. "We got

SWAT coming and they're going to knock this fucking door in!" one of them yelled. Fritz didn't want the situation to escalate or others to be hurt. He opened the door and was arrested as cops flooded in and ransacked the apartment. They ripped open stereo speakers, yanked clothes out of closets, pulled drawers out of dressers, and overturned all the beds and mattresses along with every piece of furniture not nailed down. There were no drugs in the apartment, but the cops found boxes and boxes filled with money, as well as a collection of rare guns.

The cops were proud of their day's work and boasted about their major Harlem bust. The street was locked down; 112th was packed with neighbors, lookie-loos, cops, and a SWAT team. They dragged Fritz, TyRay, and Sheila out of the building in handcuffs and drove them to the 28th Precinct, which "served" central Harlem. The hundreds of thousands of dollars in boxes was loaded onto a dolly with the rare gun collection. They were paraded into the precinct, where all eyes were on them immediately. Every cop stopped to watch the three walk in. Sheila was mortified and embarrassed as they were roughly paraded past so many gawking cops. Before being put in a cell, Sheila was taken into a bathroom by a female officer to be strip-searched.

She pleaded with the officer. "I have a bloody sanitary pad on and I'm not pulling down my panties," she said. The officer continued her search but left her panties on. It left Sheila feeling nervous, violated, and shocked. Just a few hours ago she was lying with her baby.

After the search Sheila was put in a cell in the women's holding area, while Fritz and TyRay were held in the men's area. She had never, in her whole life, wanted anything more than to get out of that cell. It was cold, dirty, dreary, and there was absolutely no privacy. She didn't want to sit on the filthy bench and wasn't going to use the stainless-steel toilet in front of everyone.

"You all right?" Fritz called out. The holding areas were in shouting distance of each other. It was noisy, but Sheila could make out Fritz's voice.

"Hell no, I ain't all right! How the fuck I'ma be all right in here!" she screamed back.

Fritz reassured her he would get her out as soon as possible. She heard him, but she couldn't process what he was saying. All she wanted was for someone to tell her she could go home. She'd just had a baby. She needed to change her pad. She needed a shower. She needed out.

Within 12 hours of her arrest, Sheila was taken into a room and questioned by detectives, who read off a list of things they claimed Fritz was into.

"We know how far you're into this," the first detective said.

"If you know all that, what are you questioning me for?" she shot back.

"Your brothers have already told us what part you played," the second detective said.

"Really? Then why I am I here, mister? Why are you questioning me if they told you what part I played?" Sheila pushed back. "I know you're taping the conversation, so tape this."

The first detective turned to the officer who'd brought her in and said, "We have a smart-ass here. Take her down to the Tombs."

The Tombs, slang for the Manhattan Detention Complex, was located in Lower Manhattan. The cells there were underground, dreary, and despairing, just like a tomb. It was a detention facility. If you were sent to the Tombs you were either waiting to see a judge about your case or waiting to be sent to prison after an indictment. No one wanted to be stuck there. There was no fresh air, bright florescent lights made it impossible to sleep well, the food was barely edible, and the bathroom stalls had no doors.

Sheila was terrified as the police once again put handcuffs on her and TyRay, and loaded them onto the crowded paddy wagon with several other detainees. Because of limited space Fritz had to wait for the next bus available. It hurt her to leave him behind. Sheila was securely strapped in her seat, but the ride was bumpy and uncomfortable with her hands cuffed behind her back. She also had sharp stomach cramps kicking in, after giving birth only several weeks ago to Howard.

When they got to the Tombs she and TyRay were separated. The men were taken to a separate area. Sheila was put in a crowded, filthy, foul-smelling holding cell with two long benches, but not enough room for everyone to sit on. There were about 15 women already inside, mostly prostitutes. It was packed—some people leaned against walls, while others slept on the floor, which was cove-red in urine and feces. It smelled like many of the women hadn't showered in days. There was a woman in the corner trying to stash drugs in her vagina. When Sheila stood against the wall two women walked over to her.

"What you in for?" the first woman asked. She shrugged.

"Don't worry. You just have to be careful when you get to Rikers… That's where things get rough, little girl," the other woman said.

Little girl? What the fuck is going on? Sheila thought. *This is not real.*

This is not happening. What the fuck am I doing in here?

A few hours later, a Rikers Island prison bus came to transport her and other detainees from the Tombs to the prison. Men and women were separated on the bus, but Sheila was relieved to see TyRay. She found it a little comforting to know she was still with family.

Then some guy in a nearby seat spoke to her.

"Shorty, shorty, lemme holla at you for a minute," he said.

"You fucking know her?" TyRay asked. "Don't be fucking saying nothing to my sister."

"Yo what the fuck is up? I'm talking to her," the guy said. "No, I'm talking to you. Don't say nothing to my sister."

Sheila gave TyRay a look that said, let it be, let it be. He met her eyes and backed down. She worried this was just a sign of things to come.

They got to Rikers in the early evening, and the two were split up again. All new arrivals were processed through the Receiving and Discharge Unit (R&D). A Correctional Officer (CO) put Sheila in a holding cell that resembled the one in the Tombs. Once her information was put into the system, she was removed from one 10 x10 cell to another. She landed in one crowded with prostitutes arguing, crack and heroin addicts nodding, and random women lying on wooden benches and the floor. Once again, a steel toilet sat in a corner for all to use publicly.

A female inmate orderly—who worked in the R&D for a few cents per hour—handed her a cup, a blanket, a short rubber toothbrush, and a small tube of toothpaste. A different orderly gave her a prison jumper and slippers and told her to put them on right there. Yet another woman, this one taller and broader than the others, walked up to Sheila licking her lips.

"Hey little mama. Ohhh, I got something for you," she said, and tried to hand her a cup of tea and a bologna sandwich. But Sheila had heard stories about prison food being spoiled, bland, spat on.

"I don't want it. I'm good. I'm good." Sheila tried to back away. "You gonna be all right, that's for sure." The woman followed as she stepped back. "I'm gonna take care of you when you come upstairs," she said.

"I'm good," Sheila repeated, pressing herself hard against the wall. She thought someone might die that night. She decided that if it was going to be her, she'd fight till there was nothing left. She'd fight to the death, but she was determined not to let this woman punk her.

Three hours later, the CO came to take Sheila to the facility's prison doctor for an examination. He sat her on a gurney, turned around, and left. A few minutes later the prison doctor walked in and announced a pap smear was needed before she was sent into population.

"You don't need to, because I'm *not* going into population. I guarantee, I'm not going there," Sheila said.

He immediately threatened her. "You can let me examine you or you can be put in medical lockup," he said. Sheila had no clue what medical lockup meant, but it didn't sound like a place she wanted to be. The lockup was actually a trip to the Special Housing Unit, also called the SHU. It was a lonely place, without phone calls or privileges. Inmates could be in the SHU for days or months without knowing when they'd go back to population.

Sheila didn't know how long she would be at Rikers Island. She didn't want to make any more trouble for herself, so she complied with the doctor.

Afterwards she was taken back to her cell for more of the waiting game. More bureaucracy. More sitting around. At 1:00 A.M., a CO told Sheila she was bailed out and could leave. It felt like forever to Sheila, having been in custody since the 2:00 P.M. raid at the apartment. She thanked God, relieved and happy to get home to her kids and a hot shower. She later found out the bail had been paid two hours earlier, but there was no response when officials were asked about the delay. Sheila had no idea that in New York State, a prison might take ten times as long to release a prisoner as it did to assign her a bed. Rikers Island's system was the worst.

Sheila was lucky; she didn't have to appear in court and the case was dropped against Fritz and TyRay. The cops had obtained their evidence through an unreasonable and illegal search, which made it inadmissible. Further, when the boxes of money were discussed in front of the judge, the figures reported were much lower than what was confiscated.

TyRay's days of hustling lasted only a short time. He never really got the hang of it, having never worked at the bottom, on the streets. Then Fritz found out he was getting high. TyRay started smoking cigarettes and weed, moved on to smoking spice joints (weed mixed with cocaine or LSD), and graduated to woolies (cigarettes mixed with PCP or crack). Fritz loved his brother and still gave him money, but no longer involved him in his drug business.

It wasn't long after one unpleasant experience that Sheila would be hit with another. On February 3rd, 1984, Sheila was visiting with her grandparents, laughing and having a good time. The phone rang, and Sheila's grandmother answered. It was LeRoy, Sheila's stepfather.

"Me and your daughter had a fight," LeRoy said to Elizabeth.

"I don't want to hear it or get in the middle of it, because y'all fight and turnaround and get back together all the time. Bye, LeRoy," she replied and hung up.

The next day, her daughter Wilhelmina was dead. Elizabeth always feared for Wilhelmina's safety after discovering the physical and mental abuse her family had endured while living with LeRoy. Knowing what was probably inevitable didn't make hearing the news any easier.

Sources said Wilhelmina's body was found in an abandoned building in the Bronx. It was not too far from the house of horrors Sheila escaped back in 1972 when she was 14. Wilhelmina's parents were asked to come and identify their daughter's body. Although Elizabeth and Claude mourned Wilhelmina, her father, at least, was relieved she could no longer be hurt by the daily abuse.

Sheila was also sad but not surprised. LeRoy finally did it; he finally killed her. He always said he would.

When a mistake at the morgue sent Sheila there—her grandparents didn't have the strength to identify their daughter twice—she was shocked at the condition of her mother's body. She had to have been dead for days. Patches of hair and teeth were missing.

Sheila felt heavy, like weights were holding her limbs down. She couldn't move or speak. All she heard was her mother saying, "I love this man more than life itself." Her emotions were conflicted. Running through her head were anger, vengeance, sadness, and then strangely, peace. Her mother's suffering was finally over.

The family tried to press charges against LeRoy, but the case was hard to prove with no witnesses or evidence that proved responsibility. Crowds of people came out and paid their respect on the cold, rainy day of Wilhelmina's funeral. The homecoming service was held at Peter Lance Funeral Home in Harlem on 132nd Street, and there were more than a hundred cars in the procession.

LeRoy didn't attend the funeral. After Wilhelmina's body was found he disappeared. Sheila was sad, but glad she didn't have to worry about her mom anymore. She could now focus her time and energy on other things. The first on her list was finding a second job. She had broken up with the first father of her two children. She was now a single mother.

Sheila wasn't single for long. She found a new man, her second daughter's father, Cooley. A high yellow man, nice-looking bald-headed, tall and lanky like a basketball player, and finally additional income. It paid the bills but was also an introduction into the drug game. Fritz liked Cooley but didn't want Sheila to be with him. Sheila was sure it had to do with Cooley bringing his drug business around her and his nieces.

Cooley was doing business with two old heads getting money named Fat Richard and Maymie. They had good heroin, and lots of money was coming through 112th to the apartment

Sheila lived in with her daughter and Cooley. Cooley would hold their money in their apartment. Sheila didn't mind at first, because things were running smoothly. Fat Richard would bring or send the heroin already cut and packaged with the name of the person Sheila was to give it to. Fat Richard's customers would either pick up the heroin or drop off money. Sheila was Cooley's bookkeeper—she kept track of everything going in and out of the apartment.

One day, the money going out of Sheila's apartment to Maymie, Fat Richard's partner, started coming up short. Sheila counted the money going out, double-checked the count, but by the time it reached Maymie's hands, the money was short. Sheila decided to stop keeping money and drugs in her house. The extra change was good, but the chances she was taking with her children in the apartment was not worth it.

Sheila was sure Maymie was taking the money. It only came up short when delivered to him. Fat Richard's kin folks, who had been getting money with him, confirmed having similar problems with Maymie.

The dope game in Harlem dried up after Fat Richard and Maymie got busted sometime in 1984-85, followed by Freddie Myers and Jesse Grey. Fritz did okay with heroin. But when crack took over, he began to reign supreme in the drug game.

For a while Sheila had one foot in and one foot out of the game. That's how Fritz wanted it, with good reason. She had children and he didn't like worrying about her or them. If it were left up to Fritz, Sheila would have never indulged in the game. At that time, successful dealers and their family members were being kidnapped for ransom.

Fritz believed the less his family knew about the ins and outs of his drug business, the safer they were. Fritz was low-key about how he moved in the streets and what he revealed to others;

only a handful of people even knew Sheila was his sister. It kept her safe in the streets and when she traveled out of New York—between nearby states and as far as Jamaica—to pick up suitcases full of money.

Fritz would give her money, but she insisted on using her own. Sheila started helping Fritz out by doing his laundry and cooking for him when Evelyn worked overtime, cleaning his house, and taking care of the dogs he fought in The Pit. She cleaned anything and everything, including the stash houses where he held supplies of cocaine and bottled crack.

Fritz's attempts to keep Sheila out of the game backfired. Sheila graduated to picking up his drug money, then to supplying her own handful of customers with keys of cocaine. The window of opportunity to make her own money cracked open more when Cooley and Sheila broke up. If Cooley's customers could not reach him, they called Sheila. She was also approached by friends in and out of town, seeking a good product or a direct introduction to Fritz—if they were one of the few people who knew they were related. Fritz never wanted to meet anyone, period, and Sheila's friends were fine using her as a go-between. They loved having a direct connect to the best cocaine on the market.

The money flow was plentiful too. Fritz would give Sheila a few thousand for every kilo she sold. The customer receiving the product would also hit her off with money to show their appreciation. Things ran smoothly every time one of her customers came in town to re-up. Sheila wasn't worried about the cops or the stickup kids, because the risks she took at first were small. She was also not concerned about the hundreds of thousands of dollars she transported through airport customs or on a plane. In the years before 9/11, surveillance wasn't a priority and airport security was minimal. There was no means to detect money or drugs at that time, no X-ray machines, no cameras, no dogs. Sheila loved her trips out of town. She stayed in the best hotels, shopped in the finest boutiques, and got waited on hand and foot.

Eventually however, the trips back and forth started to take a toll on her, and she had to pull back for the good of her children. Even after Sheila stopped traveling, Fritz would give her a key or two, looking for nothing in return. She eventually moved to Yonkers, where she expanded her small drug enterprise with the kilos Fritz gave her.

Fritz had more drugs than he knew what to do with, mostly because he was a great judge of character. He gave everybody a shot at the game; what you did with that was on you. Fritz started people off small, with a half of an eighth or a half of a key, before they would build up to getting two or three keys, called bricks. People would run off sometimes and that was the end of their story. Fritz only gave you what he could afford to lose, so he never took a huge hit. Fritz's philosophy was the less killing you had to do, the less attention you got from the cops. By then he was the Godfather of 112th Street and didn't stray too far from the block. He didn't have to—he controlled it. He was also the main supplier to dealers on nearby blocks.

As for those people who chose to run off with money or drugs, it was simple. If you did Fritz wrong, you did yourself wrong.

Queen Bee eventually found herself in that situation, according to Chucky's common-law wife, Shelagh, who witnessed it all. In the fall of 1985, Queen Bee was a different person than she had been. She was crying in the street, hollering and begging for Fritz to give her another chance. It was sad to see, but Fritz had given Queen Bee a lot of opportunities and he'd had enough of her shortchanging him. Fritz was done with her and not the least bothered by her public display. Whatever troubles Queen Bee had were now hers alone to fix. Fritz turned his back and walked away, leaving Queen Bee pleading at his back.

Two years later, a relative found Queen Bee in her apartment unresponsive on the floor. Her daughter, Trina, was on the bed nearby. Trina was mentally disabled—she was slipped some bad drugs as a teen and never fully recovered—and neighbors didn't think she understood that her mother needed help. Both women fell into serious drug use and were often high in the apartment. By the time relatives and cops arrived, Queen Bee was dead. The cops were more concerned about the drugs found in the apartment than her death. They questioned the family about possible foul play, but they were uncooperative.

The family wanted to start their own investigation. According to a neighbor, after purchasing coke from Queen Bee she saw a delivery man with a bouquet of flowers enter the apartment. It was strange since everyone knew that she was a dealer, and customers were constantly in and out buying coke. When the neighbor left, Queen Bee was in good spirits. Her daughter was there, and Queen Bee was sitting at the table sniffing coke. Less than five minutes later the neighbor heard screaming coming from Queen Bee's apartment. The neighbor hurried back downstairs to Queen Bee's apartment and found her dead.

Some say her daughter killed her after tripping out on dust. Some assumed it was a heart attack, the result of a cocaine binge, since she was a well-known user. Some thought maybe the flower man gave her a hot shot (drugs purposely spiked with poison), a hit ordered by the Lucchese crime family. Maybe they finally got revenge against Queen Bee, who testified at Vincent Papa, Sr.'s trial as a government witness. Ultimately Queen Bee died as she lived—with a lot of secrets.

The guys on 112th Street were known for having heart and getting money. They were *not* known for being the flyest dudes in Harlem or for driving the baddest cars. The block was not a runway or a car show—Fritz would not allow it. If you pulled up on the block with a flashy car or acting loud, Fritz or one of the guys getting money on 112th would tell you to move it around the corner. That's how they worked: They were low-key, under the radar. They tried not to make much noise. A lot of people came through, hoping to get a break, make a connection, or to meet Fritz, the ultimate connect. But there was no hanging out on 112th Street if you weren't visiting someone.

During Fritz's 10+ years in the drug game he never got busted or did any jail time and he made millions. He was lucky, but that wasn't the only reason. A low-level dealer on the street was a lot more likely to come in contact with the police. When you rarely touched anything personally, and people had love for someone like they did Fritz, the odds of getting busted were pretty small.

CHAPTER THIRTEEN

Black Ice "The Enforcer"

> *Black ice is a thin coat of highly transparent ice on the road or other paved surfaces. It can be slippery and very dangerous. So, it's important to recognize it and know how to react to it.*

F RITZ WAS A ONE-MAN SYNDICATE. He had no partners. He was the source of a valuable commodity and if he liked someone, he provided him an opportunity to make his money and become his own boss. He had soldiers, people who worked and were ready to die for him. He had no affiliations with any gangs, but was well protected because of his association with the Colombian cartel.

People also knew Chucky was Fritz's right and left hand. They were not related, but he was like a brother to Fritz. Chucky was Fritz's enforcer: he handled anyone foolish enough to cross him. His nickname was the Nutty One. The name was well earned.

Chucky wasn't impressed by the money, the glitz, or the glamour that came with Fritz and his drug enterprise. He kept not just one job, but often two or three at a time. He was a hardworking man who took care of his family. He also loved and mentored children. Family, brotherhood, and loyalty were important to him. Women were too, but Shelagh Coleman—his on-again off-again girlfriend and common-law wife—was his ride-or-die chick. People knew she was the Bonnie to his Clyde. They'd met when she was 18, at the Webster Bowling Alley in the Bronx.

Their attraction was immediate, but the relationship was rocky. Chucky had ten children with four women over the years, and that caused drama Shelagh wasn't prepared for. Still, they bonded over his love of dogs, like his Doberman, Red, and the pit bulls he had as pets or trained to fight. She ignored signs of his lifestyle for a long time: the guns, the men who hustled in and out of his place at all hours. Once she was clued in, she was pulled in, and he used her Bronx home as a safe house.

Life was complicated for the two. Shelagh wasn't held hostage, but he was manipulative, and she had to let him know her every move. She was under a lot of stress and anxiety for herself and her children. She was expected to keep a neat house and look out for the children, largely on her own. She knew Chucky couldn't do his work if he was worrying about his family's safety, so she took on that responsibility too. On top of that, the two got into physical fights.

She considered leaving him several times, but ultimately stayed. She knew she'd chosen his life when he taught her how to use a gun. After that, Chucky was comfortable having her around his business meetings. It was also strategic because no one knew she had a gun, or that she could handle it. She was even trusted to take notes at meetings, which she burned when the information was memorized.

Shelagh remembered a meeting Chucky had at the house with the crew. There was a dealer who wasn't paying for drugs he had gotten on consignment. The guy was a problem, always coming up short, getting high on the stash, and lying about what happened. It was one excuse after another. Fritz needed to send a message to him, the streets, and anyone else who thought he could be taken advantage of. Fritz knew early on that to maintain respect in the drug game, in the streets, and on the block sometimes meant bringing out his inner monster. Fritz had to make it clear there would be consequences.

NOTHING HAPPENED TO FRITZ WITHOUT Chucky knowing about it and vice versa. Chucky once had an issue with a guy uptown on 135th over a basketball game. Shelagh was with Chucky when several cars pulled up on the block. Chucky sent Shelagh back to the apartment while Fritz and a group of other guys emerged from their cars strapped with guns. Chucky was standing in the middle of the street. Fritz walked up and stood by his side, while Fritz's crew fell back and waited. The neighbors and children on the street all hurried indoors. It was like a scene from *Gunfight at the O.K. Corral*.[54] Thankfully no one got shot that day. As fast as the two crews came together, they just as quickly split.

It wasn't like that all the time. Fritz didn't walk around ordering hits. People had so much respect for him that it rarely got to that level. Even when dealers owed Fritz money, things rarely escalated. Fritz would take their car, let them work off the debt,

---

54   Gunfight at the O.K. Corral, Directed by John Sturges, Paramount Pictures, 1957. Film.

and then return it once they repaid his money. Fritz only resorted to violence if there was an immediate threat.

Shelagh knew when something was going down. Chucky would be serious, no smiles, all business, no time for conversation. When he looked like that, you knew to stay out of his way. Chucky always had Fritz in his scope, and was a serious undercover bodyguard. Chucky could have eyes on him without anyone knowing. They also used secret hand signals. They would see each other in passing and Fritz might say a few words or give him a sign. A few minutes later Chucky would be up on the roof with a pair of binoculars, or looking out the window, watching every move Fritz made. They were good at being covert, making it hard for anyone to know what they were thinking or what their next move would be.

Chucky never let his guard down when he was with Fritz, and he kept their arsenal in duffle bags everywhere they went. Anyone who thought that Fritz was an easy target was mistaken. That's what they were supposed to think, that Fritz was an easy vic. But if they tried to act on that misperception, they wouldn't be here very long.

CHARLES 'CHUCKY' CAINE
Fritz's Enforcer with his Common-Law Wife, Shelagh

CHAPTER FOURTEEN

The Pit

Fritz had his hand in many pots. The Pit was his dog fighting ring, managed by a friend of his named Dogman Regg (R.I.P.). He was a well-known dog trainer, whose champion purebreds dominated the city's dog rings. Many of the dogfights occurred right in the basement at 109. Dog fighting generated revenue from stud fees, admission fees, and all the gambling over whose dog would reign supreme. It was a win-win situation for Fritz, even if he didn't participate.

Ace was a teen living in Harlem when he came across Chucky walking two beautiful, healthy dogs, an American pit bull and an Akita. It would take a few chance encounters before he approached the stranger and inquired about the dogs. There were several, more small interactions before Chucky asked Ace to play on his basketball team. Being asked to play was a big deal and Ace knew it. He said yes and played half a season in the tournament held at the Courtney Callender Playground in East Harlem, named after the city's first black Deputy Commissioner of Cultural Affairs.

After the basketball season ended, Ace didn't see Chucky again until he visited Martin's Game Room, where Ace's uncle spent most of his time. Now that he knew where his mentor hung out, Ace visited his uncle more often just to see Chucky at the game room. During this time, Chucky and Ace's relationship grew. He met his family and often hung out in Chucky's house. Ace loved dogs and eventually found himself working The Pit. Chucky even gave him a few pitbull pups as gifts, that he trained and fought.

The Pit on 112th was known in all five boroughs. People brought their oversized, muscular dogs from all over the state, the country, and beyond just to fight. A well-known WBC lightweight champion boxer came from St. Kitts, shipping his dogs. Customers bet untold amounts of money, often on a whim.

One night a Harlem resident, Mr. Uptown, came through The Pit with a friend to check it out. He was dripping with lots of jewelry and thick pockets filled with money. He boasted of their dogs, which were conveniently not with them. They argued that The Pit's dogs were nothing compared to theirs and bet $500 for a match. They were laughed at.

Big Gee (R.I.P.), who was working that night, bet $1,000 to have fun with them. Mr. Uptown then bet $10,000 and expected to be victorious. But legendary trainer Dogman Regg was in the room, and Fritz, observing quietly from across the room, felt he was being disrespected. Fritz bet $50,000 "or however much you want." His statement, left open ended, shocked onlookers and the two men into silence. They left with their tails between their legs.

They never fought dogs to the death in The Pit and Dogman Regg was always on standby if a dog got seriously hurt. He was an excellent trainer, and in another life, he could've been an incredible veterinarian. He had a well-trained, cock diesel pit bull named Mad Maxx. Dogman Regg would walk the streets with Mad Maxx unleashed. He was great at following commands and waited for Dogman Regg when he went into stores and ran errands. He'd ignore everything and everyone, focusing on the door until Dogman Regg came out. Maxx could play hide and seek, and sometimes carried small boom boxes and even logs. Once, Dogman Regg emerged from a grocery store and found four men teasing Maxx, with one command the dog was viciously growling as if to attack. The four men were so scared they did as told, and stood against a wall with their pants around their ankles until someone found Fritz to defuse things. Dogman Regg thought it was hilarious.

Dogman died in 2010 of appendicitis at the age of 47. His premature death was all the more tragic, as it was rumored that the federal government had reached out to him shortly before his death with a job offer. They'd heard of his dog training skills and wanted him to help train their drug-and bomb-sniffing K-9s.

REGINALD "DOGMAN REGG" JOHNSON

DOGMAN REGG WITH SAMPSON
Breed: Rottweiler

DOGMAN REGG WITH BADNEWS
Breed: Neapolitan Mastiff

GEERARD X AKA BIG GEE WITH LL COOL J
Dapper Dan's Fashion Boutique in Harlem

CHAPTER FIFTEEN

An Ace In The Hole

This phrase originates from the game of poker, where a card dealt face down and kept hidden is called a 'hole card', the most favorable card being the Ace.

AFTER TWO YEARS OF WORKING The Pit with Chucky, Ace decided to quit. His second job at the supermarket didn't allow him enough time to do both. Besides that, someone had told the store manager that Ace was selling crack out of his store. He denied the accusations, but his guilt got the better of him. It was easier for him to move on and work full-time for Chucky and Fritz on 129th Street and Madison. Ace moved crack as fast as he got it from Chucky—the demand for the substance never stopped, never slowed. At one point Chucky was giving Ace ounces at a time from his coke stash.

"You need to go talk to Fritz the way you movin," Chucky

instructed him. Ace did so and was immediately refused. Fritz didn't want Ace hustling like that. He felt personally responsible for the younger man and wanted to keep him out of the game. It went on for weeks—Ace would ask, Fritz would say no.

Ace was frustrated; he had a child to take care of, and what little money he had was all going to carfare to and from 112th Street. Fritz eventually gave in. Ace took 125g of coke, cooked it up into crack, put it on the streets, and brought Fritz back $2,000 the next day. Fritz was surprised how fast he turned the drugs over for a first-timer. Fritz was forced to concede that Ace was a good earner. He'd underestimated the young man; he sold the product fast and re-upped often. Ace slowly took over three abandoned buildings on the block and made them drug spots. Within four short months, Ace had saved up enough cash to purchase his drugs outright.

"Just hold onto your paper and build," Fritz advised. He knew Ace was anxious to prove himself and make a name, but he believed in being cautious. People made mistakes when they rushed.

Ace was a smart hustler and used his customers to help grow his business. He would pay them in crack to check out the competition. This way Ace gained their loyalty and was able to keep ahead of his fellow dealers. If they were selling vials for $5, he sold his pink tops for $4, packing the crack vial to the rim. He also devised a marketing plan—every crackhead who brought five customers would get a $4 pink top for free. This was ideal for customers low on cash.

There were other days Ace had his workers give product away for free, just to attract more customers. He even came up with a jingle for the workers to say when they sold his crack: "Pink is out. Pink is out. We on. We on hard, tall, and strong. We on in the basement," they would repeat, indicating what their product is and where to purchase it. Ace's marketing campaign was a huge success. It created such long lines of people wanting to buy crack that it sparked the cops' interest, which led workers to disperse the crowds.

In response, Fritz stepped it up. Ace was getting a key every three to four days and bringing in $30,000 a day, $180,000 a week. His spot was open twelve hours a day, six days a week, with six guys working the day shift and six working overnight. Ace had the east side of Harlem on lock.

Things were good and money was plentiful, but their success would eventually bring out the haters and later, the police.

IN THE DRUG GAME THERE were always challenges, many of them life or death. Ace had a low tolerance for nonsense and was quick to pull a trigger.

He once ran into a problem on his block with a dealer named Pork, a name given to him when he was young—he was a bit on the chunky side. Pork had just gotten out of prison and wanted to reclaim 129th. One morning Ace's people got to work, only to find the door locked and the spot taken over by Pork's workers. Ace came to the block to straighten the matter out. He knocked on the door and the dealer opened the makeshift window they served customers out of.

"What you want?" the worker asked.

Ace stuck his Taurus PT99 semi-automatic through the window into the man's face.

"You have three seconds to come out or I'm gonna come in and kill you," Ace said.

The men left, but soon returned with Pork and his partner, Pigeon Head. Pork had just come home from prison and had some size on him. Pigeon Head was married to Fritz's cousin.

"You can't be pointing guns in a dude's face," Pork said.

"And, you can't be putting dudes in my fucking spot. Who the fuck y'all niggers think ya is?" Ace responded.

"It's all right to sell on the block, but not on the Ave," Pigeon Head said.

The three men went back and forth on territory. The whole time Ace argued back and forth with Pork and Pigeon Head, he still held his Taurus PT99. The bickering was getting to him. He was seconds away from ending the conversation by shooting them both when he locked eyes with three nuns walking past the men. Believers in miracles witnessed one happen that day.

The nuns were from All Saints Catholic Church, on the corner of 129th and Madison—their home was on the same street. The nuns knew Ace, knew what he did on the block. They also knew he kept a low profile, and kept the block quiet. People copped their drugs and left. Ace had his workers keep the block clean, free of garbage, and respectable for its residents.

As Ace stood there with the gun in his hand, he believed he could hear their silent pleas. *Don't kill those men. Don't kill them.* Ace slowly tucked the gun under one arm. The nuns passed the trio and entered a brownstone a few feet away. Maybe it was divine intervention: Ace didn't pull the trigger, and the nuns didn't call the police. Pork and Pigeon Head left, but nothing had been worked out.

Ace went home to relax and think about how he would kill Pork and Pigeon Head. He felt he had to. He felt they were playing him because he was younger than the other dealers, and newer in the game. Fritz came in and found him sitting on the couch, unusually quiet. He knew Ace was plotting, and plotting never ended well.

"What happened?" Fritz asked. Ace brushed off the altercation at first, but then told Fritz the truth. He also told him his plan for revenge. Fritz didn't want him to become a killer and told him to focus on his money.

Feeling the need to intervene, Fritz went uptown to talk directly to Pork. They came to an agreement, but ultimately it didn't help Pork. His aggressive approach to life and people created problems for him in the streets. Two weeks after Ace and Pork resolved their difference, Pork was murdered in a cab on 125th Street.

In the late eighties, the keys were flowing and the money was growing for Ace. Fritz was giving him twenty keys at a time. At the start of the nineties it shot up to fifty keys.

"Make deals, but don't mess with anyone new," Fritz instructed him. More than ever, it was best to keep outsiders at a distance. A lot of people wanted to get close to Fritz and had hidden agendas, but no one could turn Ace against him.

Money was coming fast. Ace would drop off shopping bags full of cash to Fritz. Ace never counted it, just dropped the cash off and let Fritz deal with it all, like something out of *Scarface*.

Fritz showed Ace the books one day and to Ace's surprise, he'd made close to a million dollars that week.

A few years earlier, in 1987, Ace was on the rooftop of a four-story brownstone on 127th Street working on his target practice. Ace, his cousin Shooter, and a friend, Tony were taking turns shooting at tin cans. He had his Taurus PT99 on him and they both had Mossberg 500 series shotguns—so all three froze when they heard the police sirens coming up the block.

"Hide your guns in the house and I'll keep the cops at bay," Ace told his cousin.

The guys took off quickly. Ace looked down from the roof and saw cops hurrying out of squad cars. It looked like all of the 25th Precinct and the Housing Police from Drew Hamilton Houses—called the Hamilton projects—were on the scene.

He just needed enough time for his guys to stash their guns and for him to get away. Ace let off several warning shots, hoping the commotion would delay the cops. He ran to his cousin's top-floor apartment nearby, but the door was locked. He headed down to the front door, never letting go of his gun. A cop was headed up the same stairs with a .38-caliber revolver in his hand.

Ace and the cop met face-to-face. They stared at each other in silence for a brief second, neither knowing the other's thoughts. But they guessed they both wanted to go home and see their children. They both wanted to live to fight another day.

Without a word, the cop turned his back on Ace and flew back down the stairs. Ace spun on his heel and ran back up to the rooftop. He was trapped up there, with cop cars lit up and swarming the block below him. An adjoining brownstone was locked, the fire escape covered by police. His only option was a jump to another brownstone, and if he missed, it was a four-story drop. Ace hesitated. This wasn't something he planned for. At that moment the cops burst through the rooftop door with their guns drawn.

"Drop the gun!" an officer yelled.

Ace ignored the cops, focusing only on escape. He saw a tall tree with long branches and thought maybe he could make it. He didn't have much time to think and, in that instance, he decided to jump.

He leaped off the roof and threw the semi-automatic in the opposite direction. Ace made it to the tree, but lost his grip and fell four stories to the concrete below, dislocating his shoulder and breaking his wrist. The cops quickly surrounded him. Ace was arrested and taken to jail, with bail set at $15,000.

Ace stood before the judge with a tired court-appointed attorney next to him. He had a cast on one foot and one arm was in a sling, and he didn't feel great about his chances. But before the judge could speak, a well-dressed attorney Ace had never seen before entered the courtroom and walked directly to him.

"I'll be taking over his case," Irvin Levine, the new high-profile Jewish lawyer said.

Ace was just as confused as the judge until he saw a familiar face in the courtroom. It was Peggy, Fritz's girl Friday, signaling to him that this attorney with the expensive suit was sent by Fritz. Ultimately there were no indictments for the rooftop incident. The cops couldn't find Ace's gun, and that was all they had. Ace never forgot that, nor the day that sealed their brotherhood when Fritz's apartment became Ace's safe house.

It was 1988, Ace was living on 116th Street in a tenement building on Park Avenue. The cops were in pursuit of a man who had run into the building with a gun. Ace was emptying garbage when the cops ran up the stairs and saw him in the hallway. The cops assumed the gunman had run into Ace's apartment and pointed their guns at Ace.

"Freeze!" a cop yelled.

"Oh shit!" Ace responded. He didn't move.

Killer, Ace's pit bull, had been trained to sense when Ace was in danger by the tone of his voice and body language. Killer ran to Ace's side and started growling at the cops. The cops backed away when Killer appeared. Ace quickly pulled the dog back inside with him and shut the door. He had just picked up four keys from Fritz and had several guns in the apartment.

Ace needed to get rid of the drugs and guns before the cops kicked in the door. Ace threw an AK-47 and a police riot shotgun out of his bedroom window. The guns landed on a pile of garbage between two buildings, in an area impossible for the cops or sanitation to reach. He left behind the dog, the drugs, whatever money was in the house, a 9mm behind the TV set, a MAC-11 behind the speaker, and a .22 in the refrigerator. He then climbed out of the bedroom window and down the fire escape.

Ace managed to escape the cops but needed someplace to lay low fast. He called Fritz from a payphone, understandably upset. He picked up Ace and rode back to the crime scene. From a distance, Fritz saw crowds of cops and police vans. Ace found a dealer who hustled in the building who confirmed that the cops were in Ace's apartment. Killer had been placed in the back of one of their vans.

Ace knew that after all the drugs, money, and guns found in the apartment, he couldn't go back. Now he also owed Fritz $64,000 for all the cocaine lost in the incident.

"Don't sweat that. Don't worry about what you lost, as long as you can make money going forward," Fritz told him, much to Ace's relief.

Now Ace just needed a place to stay. Staying with his mom or other relatives after the incident wasn't a good idea; the cops might find mail leading them to him. Fritz suggested that Ace stay with him at 109 until things cooled down; it was very clear Fritz wanted Ace off the street for a while.

Fritz had the right idea, as the next day, Ace's name and the incident were mentioned publicly on local radio station 1010 WINS. Fritz's place became Ace's safe house, and the cops never traced him there. Fritz made sure Ace had whatever he needed. However, the only outside communication Ace had was with Fritz. It would be four months before he could resurface and conduct business again. The men's brotherhood naturally grew from there and their bond made them as thick as thieves.

Their closeness created some jealousy and tension with the other workers and dealers on 112th. Ace was considered an outsider, and his quick rise to insider status ruffled some feathers. Ace was still somewhat new, yet Fritz let him all the way in on his business dealings. Clearly Fritz found him to be a stand-up guy, reliable, and trustworthy.

One day Ace asked Fritz, "Why you trust me so much?"

"That closet I told you not to go in when you first moved in… I know you went in there," Fritz said.

The closet was where Fritz stashed his money; he kept millions of dollars inside. It was unlocked but rigged. There had been many opportunities for Ace to rip Fritz off, but he never did. Fritz would confirm that Ace had been in the closet, but hadn't touched the cash. Ace passed the test. Fritz knew Ace was someone he could trust and rely on. He needed to be trusted 100% if he was going to meet Fritz's connect.

Fritz would eventually give him even more responsibilities. He would often send Ace to handle his business with the connect, who grew fond of Ace and invited him out to a restaurant they owned on City Island. Ace visited so often with friends that they'd set up a special table just for them.

Fritz was exposing Ace to more of the business, and that business was growing every day.

"We gonna need a bigger vehicle to move these drugs," Fritz said to him one day.

Fritz had been transporting drugs in a 1987 Maxima. Now it could no longer fit the increasing amounts of cocaine he was transporting weekly. After Fritz's comment, Ace surprised him with a customized Dodge Ram 250 van.

Ace had the routine to pick up or drop off money down to a science. He would drive to the connect in the Bronx and call Fritz. The connect would come out, Ace would give him the keys to the van and head back to Harlem by train. Fritz would get a call when it was time to pick up the van. Fritz and Ace would return to the Bronx and pick up the Dodge, now loaded with six large boxes filled with bricks of cocaine. There were at least 50 kilos to a box, 300 keys in total—that's what they brought in weekly. Fritz would wait a few days, then distribute the kilos to their workers with Ace's help.

Ace handled hundreds of keys of coke and truckloads of money, and eventually he would handle pickups directly from the Colombians. Fritz respected him. He'd found his ace in the hole.

ACE AKA KING MARIO
Fritz's Right-Hand Man

CHAPTER SIXTEEN

Thirty Silver Coins

> *I speak not of you all; I know whom I have chosen: but that the scripture may be fulfilled, He that eateth bread with me hath lifted up his heel against me.*
>
> —JOHN 13:18

FAST MONEY IS NOT ALWAYS good money, but it's a means to an end. Most would rather have it than not, and would do anything to get it. "It's the root of all evil," mamas would say to their children.

Before Ace came on the scene, JD was Fritz's number one. He was local, from the neighborhood, and Fritz had known him a long time. Fritz depended on JD to handle various business transactions and pickups from the connect. It was in the early '80s that Fritz noticed JD moving differently. He was concerned—he had to be able to rely on his people through and through. The game demanded loyalty at all times.

One day Sheila came downstairs to visit Evelyn and walked in on Fritz cursing and slapping JD around in the living room. JD wasn't a small guy, he had a slim muscular frame, but size didn't matter under Fritz's reign. If someone respected him they just accepted what he dished out. Fritz was a mild-mannered guy, so Sheila knew it had to be serious.

Fritz met JD on the block—JD lived with his family across the street from Fritz. He also hung out in Martin's Game Room with neighborhood teens; it was likely how the two met.

JD was there in the beginning of the crack era, when Fritz was getting 500 kilos a month. Fritz needed a crew of trustworthy people to help distribute it fast. JD was in the right place at the right time. His baby face and quiet demeanor sometimes made him invisible on the block, which attracted Fritz. While Fritz positioned JD in a high-level position without worry, however, many on the block had reservations. People thought him to be sneaky, two-faced, and too soft to be promoted to boss or second-in-command. However, they respected Fritz's decision and kept their opinions to themselves. Fritz knew the rumors and had some reservations of his own, but JD had the most sense and was low-key compared to the other dealers on his team.

In the drug game, sometimes there were so-called droughts, when no drugs could be found for various reasons (crops went bad, or the DEA made a huge bust). In 1989, Fritz's drug shipment got caught up on a barge on the Hudson River for a couple of months.[55] Fritz needed to keep things afloat, so to speak. He decided to use his plan B, his Bahamas connections, but his money

---

[55] Mydans, Seth. "Agents Seize 20 Tons of Cocaine In Raid on Los Angeles Warehouse." The New York Times Archives, 30 September 1989, Section 1, Page 1, https://www.nytimes. com/1989/09/30/us/agents-seize-20-tons-of-cocaine-in-raid-on-los-angeles-warehouse.html.

was tied up on the streets. JD, who had known Fritz the longest, never offered him assistance. Ace, however, stepped up immediately and gave Fritz money to purchase coke from the Bahamas. He helped Fritz put the whole deal together. This included paying all expenses for the young women Fritz used as drug mules. He handed them tickets and they flew to the Bahamas.

JD eventually showed his true colors. New York City suffered another drug drought. No one had any cocaine and customers were restless. Dealers were pushing hard to get product in any way they could. JD knew about Fritz's Bahamas coke connection and saw the opportunity to make a move on his own without his permission.

JD sent a guy to the Bahamas to get several keys of bottled liquid coke. Drug mules would often smuggle the drug in condoms, shampoo or liquor bottles. But the guy got nervous and panicked coming through customs. He tossed the bottles—four kilos of liquid cocaine— in the airport. This blunder cost Fritz his connect in the Bahamas.

Sheila thought Fritz would reprimand JD for this. She had witnessed him slap JD around once for a much smaller mistake.

Fritz didn't want to be bothered with JD after that, but the truth was, JD knew Fritz's entire operation. Fritz didn't want to involve new people in his business. It took time to train them, time to build trust, and there was too much at stake. He decided to keep JD working despite his blunder. At least with his enemies close he could keep an eye on them. It was at this point that Fritz began grooming Ace to be his number one.

Ace and JD never really got along. They never did business, but Ace once loaned him $5,000 when asked, probably out of respect for Fritz. He tried to make friends with JD when he was first put on, but quickly saw through the phony smile plastered on his face around Fritz.

JD would eventually take a back seat to Ace in Fritz's drug business. Things were changing quickly in the business and JD had no control over it. In the end, he had no respect for, or loyalty to, Fritz. It became a matter of "I'm gonna get mine, while I can." JD's bad attitude started to show. There was a time when Fritz fell ill and very weak. At that point he could barely stand and often needed assistance.

JD's girl saw Fritz on 112th Street. She blamed Fritz for JD staying out late most nights and sometimes not even coming home. She rolled up on Fritz yelling and causing a scene. Fritz told her to get lost. He was in the middle of a business transaction and the last thing he needed was cops pulling up, thinking it was a domestic dispute. When the girl told JD what happened, she said that Fritz had disrespected her, which was far from the truth. JD confronted Fritz, thinking he was defending his girl's honor, words were exchanged and then blows. It was said the JD got the better of Fritz that day because he was sick, visibly weak and suffering from pneumonia, which JD knew. Again, he had seized the window of opportunity and taken advantage of Fritz.

JD, who betrayed Fritz for financial gain or "coin" was just like Judas Iscariot, who betrayed Jesus for 30 silver coins. He pretended to be his friend and follower, but as it turned out he was only a deceiver.

1990s

CHAPTER SEVENTEEN

The Wild Cowboys Dead or Alive

THE FLOW OF MONEY AND drugs on the streets of New York City was plentiful. Depending on the hustle, some made more money than others. And some were walking targets for extortionists, blackmailers, and kidnappers, like the Wild Cowboys, a ruthless set of individuals organized by Steven Palmer from the Bronx.[56] They posed as police and primarily targeted drug dealers, who at times committed murders in the wake of their kidnappings. Then there was the Preacher Crew, led by Clarence "Preacher" Heatley. He was called Preacher for his speechmaking power. He was also called "The Black Hand of

---

56   (56a) Hevesi, Dennis. "9 Men Posing as Police Are Indicted in 3 Murders." The New York Times Archives, 30 September 1992, Section B, Page 3, https://www.nytimes. com/1992/09/30/nyregion/9-men-posing-as-police-are-indicted-in-3-murders.html.

Death," so intimidated and feared by other Harlem dealers that they paid him up to $30,000 just to be left alone.[57]

In December 1989, Richard "Richie Rich" Porter, a crack dealer and friend of Fritz's, came knocking on his door. Richie's 12-year-old brother, Donnell, had been kidnapped while walking to school near 132nd Street. The kidnappers demanded $500,000 for his release, which Richie Rich allegedly couldn't pay. It was rumored that Richie Rich had met with several other Harlem dealers to borrow $300,000 in cash that he couldn't cover for the ransom. It was a meeting Fritz did not attend. Instead he gave Richie Rich a Louis Vuitton back full of cash to move out of Harlem temporarily and 30 "free" kilos of cocaine that he could flip. No strings attached. With the money Richie Rich generated from selling the coke, he could afford Donnell's ransom.

Richie Rich met with Fritz again and Ace was also present, this time on 100th Street and Fifth Avenue.

"The streets talk, Rich. You'll find out more if you fall back off the scene. Take a step back to clear your head, so you can think. It could be anybody watching your every move. They could be monitoring you right now," Fritz advised. Rumors were racing throughout Harlem over the kidnapping. It wasn't unusual back then for drug dealers to be extorted for money, but the kidnapping of a young boy was. People hinted that the kidnappers might even be known to the family, someone they would trust, and Donnell would trust.

Richie agreed but had no intention of following Fritz's advice. He was too scared for his younger brother, so laying low wasn't

---

[57] Weiser, Benjamin. "Suspect Wanted to Talk; Now He May Face Execution." The New York Times Archives, 2 April 1998, Section B, Page 1, https://www.nytimes.com/1998/04/02/ nyregion/suspect-wanted-to-talk-now-he-may-face-execution.html.

an option. Richie Rich stayed out in the open talking to people, asking questions and bringing attention to himself. Without cover or someone watching his back he could not know where the threat was coming from. He had put himself in a position for the kidnappers to monitor his every move.

Richie Rich's carelessness put him and Donnell in greater danger but worse, he'd put Fritz, who had given him 30 kilos of cocaine, under a microscope. Fritz told Richie not to call him from the house phone once the kidnapping made national news and attracted the attention of the Feds. But Richie was panicked and desperate. He called Fritz at home on a payphone, which led the Feds right to Fritz's door on 108th Street, where he was living with Lauren and their sons. The FBI agents questioned the man at the door about Fritz, not realizing Fritz stood before them. He was able to get rid of them, but now Fritz was concerned they were monitoring the building or questioning neighbors. He also knew he had to have another talk with Richie, who had put his whole operation in danger.

Richie Rich never got the chance to pay the ransom. On January 4th, 1990, his body was found near Orchard Beach Park.[58] He had been shot several times in the head and chest. No one knew at the time who killed him, but the two grand cops found in his pocket ruled out robbery.

Fritz's gut told him that Richie Rich's murder had something to do with his 30 kilos of cocaine. He had people in the streets looking for answers. Rumors swirled that Richie Rich's lieutenant

---

[58] McKinley Jr., James C. "Missing Boy: Drug Trade Hits Again." The New York Times Archives, 6 Jan 1990, Section 1, Page 27, https://www.nytimes.com/1990/01/06/nyregion/missing-boy-drug-trade-hits-again.html.

to his drug enterprise, Wayne O, might have some information about Richie and the missing cocaine.

Fritz and Ace searched the streets of Harlem for Wayne O, eventually spotting him driving down Lenox Avenue. They chased him down but couldn't catch him. Fritz later found out that Wayne O was hiding out with his girlfriend at her mother's house on 131st Street.

Fritz showed up at the mother's door, but she refused to give up any information. Turned out his visit was enough to scare Wayne O into reaching out. He confirmed that Alberto "Alpo" Martinez, Richie's partner, had the 30 keys. Richie Rich had given Alpo the keys to sell in DC, as he couldn't move them with the Feds watching. Alpo was making a lot of money in DC and Richie Rich knew he would have no problem selling the coke. The street value for a key in the early '90s was $23,000. Richie wasn't looking to make a profit, just to flip them fast to get his ransom cash together. Knocking off the street value price and selling super low at $10,000 per key would have gotten him the $300,000 he needed.

A meeting was set up between Fritz and Alpo on 132nd Street at a mutual friend's candy store. Alpo was young and good looking, known for being flashy and flamboyant with his clothes, cars, and jewelry. He was such a character in Harlem that he was immortalized in the movie *Paid in Full* by uptown rapper Cam'ron.[59] He was also widely known as a talker.

Alpo arrived with four guys from DC to find Fritz already there. Alpo then opened his jacket to reveal a gun tucked into his waistband.

"You know I come prepared," Alpo said.

Fritz had also come prepared. Ace and several shooters were

---

[59] *Paid in Full*, Directed by Charles Stone III. Miramax Films, 2002. Film.

strategically set up outside the store. If Fritz didn't come out, Alpo and his DC crew wouldn't make it out either.

The conversation then went back and forth between the two.

They each lost and gained ground, heating up as they negotiated.

Fritz knew the conversation was over when Alpo said, "Fritz, you gave those keys to Richie Rich and a dead man can't pay."

Fritz left the candy store, chalking up the 30 keys as a loss. Alpo was so bold and cocky that he hoped that Fritz would continue doing business as usual after Richie Rich's death. It was clear from the conversation that Alpo had no intention of paying the ransom to free Donnell, who was still missing and now missing a finger courtesy of his kidnappers. Alpo wanted to be the head man in charge and Richie Rich's kilos provided him that opportunity.

Fritz never cared for Alpo's loudmouth and splashy ways. He had never done business with him, and after how things went down with him in the candy store, he knew he would never do business with him. Alpo was too mouthy, too boastful, all the things that got dealers busted or killed.

Fritz was right: Alpo's days were numbered. On November 6, 1991, Alberto "Alpo" Martinez was arrested on cocaine distribution charges in Northern Virginia and wanted for questioning in drug-related killings from Washington, DC to New York.[60] To reach a deal Alpo turned government witness, snitching on several DC drug dealers as well as his personal hitman, Wayne "Silk" Perry. Perry would later go to jail for life. Finally, Alpo confessed

---

60   Hedges, Chris. "Street Tales, Grisly and Raw: Grim True-Crime Magazine Hits Home With Inmates." The New York Times Archives, 6 December 1999, https://www.nytimes.com/1999/12/06/nyregion/street-tales-grisly-and-raw-grim-true-crime-magazine-hits-home-with-inmates.html

to murdering Richie Rich for the cocaine. He was the one who'd dumped Richie's body at Pelham Bay Park.

On January 28, 1990, three weeks after Richie Rich's body was found, Donnell Porter's body was also found in Pelham Bay Park, wrapped in plastic bags.[61] The ransom had gone unpaid, even after an amputated finger had been sent to his family. Donnell pleaded with them on the phone for someone to help him. It was a tragedy, and a preventable one. Even worse, a few years later, Richie and Donnell's uncle, John "Apple" Porter, an affiliate of the notorious and highly feared Preacher Crew, admitted to taking part in Donnell's kidnapping and murder. Apple may have sealed his nephew's fate, as he wore no mask and could be identified. A mother had to bury two sons as a result.

The first attempt to extort Fritz directly was in the spring of 1990. Fritz and Ace were on their way to see the Bronx connect. Whenever Fritz was out late handling business, he checked on Lauren and his son, who were visiting her mother. While Fritz and Ace rode up to the Bronx to see the connect, he called Lauren several times from his mobile phone, but there was no answer. He got a page, then quickly turned the car around, heading to Lauren's mother's house up the street from 109.

"Some stickup kids were waiting in the hallway when Lauren got home, and forced her to open the door at gunpoint," Fritz explained to Ace on the way.

"Stickup kids?" Ace repeated.

"Yeah. They panicked when they heard the phone ringing and ran off with some money and jewelry."

---

[61] Lorch, Donatella. "Body of a Boy Found in Bags On Bronx Path" The New York Times Archives, January 30, 1990, Section B, Page 3, https://www.nytimes.com/1990/01/30/nyregion/body-of-a-boy-found-in-bags-on-bronx-path. html.

"She all right?"

"Yeah, just shook up a bit, but she's good."

The next day Fritz was sitting on the block on 112th when a messenger, unknown to him and sent by the Wild Cowboys, got out of a black Jeep to hand him a package. He then retreated near the Jeep, where the driver was idling.

In the package was a note and a ring the stickup kids had taken from the house. It happened to be Lauren's favorite, and when Fritz saw the jewelry he turned to Ace and yelled two words: "Get 'em!"

The messenger jumped into the Jeep but was grabbed by Ace before the driver could pull off. Two cops saw the scuffle and ran to intervene, separating the two fighting men. The Jeep driver was dismissed, but the cops detained Ace and the messenger to sort out the details of the altercation. They quickly grew frustrated as neither side would say anything at all. Eventually both were let go with a warning.

"I hope this is over. The next time we're not going to let ya off so easy," one of the cops said.

The messenger hurried down into the nearest train station on Lenox Avenue headed uptown. When the cops left, a few guys from 112th who'd been watching from a distance ran down into the station after him. When he realized the 112th Street guys saw him, the messenger ran down the subway platform, jumped the track, and raced into the tunnel. Transit cops were alerted, and they cleared the station and alerted patrolmen.

The cops escorted the messenger out of the subway station and pointed him to the Lexington Avenue train station. As soon as the cops were gone, the 112th Street guys continued their chase. The messenger headed toward the East Side, cutting through Foster Projects/King Towers. This large housing project was known for its legendary street ballers and visiting NBA players at celebrity basketball games, including Metta World Peace, Walter Berry, Dominique Wilkins, and Joakim Noah. It was also infamous for its many escape routes, and the messenger used them to escape the 112th Street crew.

Henry Clemente, known as Hen Dog, was a teenager from the Bronx. He would often visit his stepfather at their family's store, Harris Grocery, and then hang out on the block or at Martin's Game Room with other teens. He'd watch all the drugs, money, expensive cars, and beautiful women that streamed in and out of 112th. It didn't take long for him to figure out that all the activity was the result of one man, Richard "Fritz" Simmons.

Hen Dog never had to turn to the streets; his family was well-off. They owned two businesses—the grocery store on 112th, and Harris Cleaners near Fritz's building at 109. They also owned a house in the Soundview section of the Bronx, where his brother Christopher was a good student and athlete with a promising future. There was something about the street life, though, that hooked Hen Dog. Maybe it was all the respect and attention Fritz received that hooked him: he craved that sort of attention and wanted to be a part of that life. He wanted something from life that his family's money couldn't buy. Hen Dog was an ambitious young man looking to get close to Fritz, and when the opportunity presented itself, he seized it without hesitation.

After hearing of Fritz's run-in with the Wild Cowboys and their messenger, Hen Dog wanted to prove his loyalty and prove himself worthy of a spot in Fritz's inner circle. He started carrying a gun wherever he went. A few weeks later, Hen Dog spotted the messenger in a restaurant in the Bronx and shot and killed him. Fritz never ordered that hit.

Hen Dog was running wild, Evelyn was down south, and Sheila was living in Yonkers with her children. Fritz thought they'd be far from the danger that threatened him and his family, but it wasn't far enough from the people looking to extort him. Sheila noticed a guy with dreadlocks had been watching her for a few days as she walked in and out of the building. Sheila pointed him out to a neighbor, someone who'd been in the building for years. The neighbor didn't know him either, which made her nervous.

Sheila became more aware of her surroundings and the people around her as she went about her day. She was doubly nervous because it was just her and the children living in Yonkers: They were alone up there otherwise. She noticed the guy with dreadlocks again when she went to the store late one evening. He walked in a few minutes after she did and pretended to browse before finally confronting her.

"Are you Fritz's sister?" he asked. "Who? No," she responded. "You look just like him," he said. They were alone.

Thoughts of what happened to Richie Rich and Donnell ran through Sheila's mind and made her even more nervous. Why would a complete stranger come up to her asking questions about her brother? The area she lived in Yonkers was quiet and secluded. Sometimes the fog rolling off the Hudson was so thick, it could be difficult to see who was in front of you. And it wasn't like Harlem—people didn't hang outside at night, which made it very easy for someone wanting to grab you off the street.

Sheila's sixth sense told her to get the hell out of there. She quickly left the store, hurried back home, and called her brother. Fritz came up the very next day, along with two Colombians wearing trench coats and carrying sawed-off shotguns underneath. They went down to the strip on Riverdale Avenue, where young people and addicts hung out and dealers sold their merchandise.

Fritz made sure people saw him, and not surprisingly, many knew who he was as he addressed the group of dealers on the strip.

Looking each one in the eye, with the stone-faced Colombians standing quietly by his side, Fritz said, "If anything happens to my sister or one of my nieces or nephews, I'm coming back up here." He never raised his voice, and he didn't threaten anyone outright. His tone spoke volumes.

Sheila never had a problem after that.

Meanwhile, Fritz still had the attention of the Wild Cowboys. Since their attempt at his girl's apartment and the handling of the note, it was only a matter of time before they'd try to strike again. The Cowboys were quickly gaining a reputation with their use of intimidation and violence to expand their territory from Washington Heights in upper Manhattan into the South Bronx. Their crack operation often used children as young as 12 to carry drugs and act as lookouts. They also developed a vicious reputation as being quick to kill anyone, especially members accused of disloyalty.

According to an article in the *New York Times,* cops believed the kidnapping ring had two components. One was what they dubbed "the crew." It included men from the South Bronx involved in the lucrative drug trade, men who scouted for victims to kidnap. The other, the "cowboys," were comprised of men from New Jersey, Westchester, and Rockland County, who carried out the kidnappings. The ring had an elaborate operation. Equipped with badges and guns, the men posed as police officers and staged phony arrests to kidnap drug dealers off the street and hold them for ransom. Shortly after Christmas in 1990, the Wild Cowboys snatched Alvin Goings, a competing drug dealer, from a laundromat he operated in the Bronx. Alvin's people came up with a ransom of $650,000 before he was released. He was lucky. The Wild Cowboys were known to be so vicious that its members stood on rooftops using people playing in the park for target practice. They once shot a college student to death on the West Side Highway because he cut them off at an entrance ramp. In two other kidnappings by the Wild Cowboys, the victims were assaulted but escaped. In one case, a man was captured at a garage in Yonkers, taken to a motel in New Jersey, where he was tortured with a staple gun. Though handcuffed to a chair, he managed to break loose and escape. In the second kidnapping, a man was taken from a barbershop in Manhattan, driven to a garage, handcuffed to a pipe, and beaten. Later that day, he was shot and wounded as he escaped. A third kidnapping victim, a Bronx dealer named David Crumpler, was taken from his restaurant and held hostage for $750,000. Despite torturing Crumpler with a blackjack, a stun gun, and a staple gun. As a result of no ransom ever being paid, Crumpler was shot to death, his handcuffed body was later found dumped in a vacant lot in the Bronx.

But the Wild Cowboys still believed they could catch their ulti-mate prize and biggest payday with Fritz, the million-dollar man, New York's king of kingpins…or someone close to him. Unfortunately, the opportunity that was botched twice in the past would lead to a third and an even greater failure for the Wild Cowboys.

One evening, the Wild Cowboys trailed Fritz throughout the neighborhood and stopped him on a street corner on 116th and Morningside Avenue. They attempted to "arrest" him, but Fritz had heard of the attacks on other dealers and knew their tactics.

The Wild Cowboys' ringleader insisted Fritz was under arrest and attempted to drag him into their car.

"*Yo, help…help! They're not cops!*" Fritz yelled to the black and brown people sitting on their stoops.

The people on the block were confused, but the shouting made them nosey and they slowly surrounded the Wild Cowboys.

Fritz had attracted unwanted attention and it made them nervous. Rather than be exposed, they let Fritz go and fled the scene.[62]

After the latest failed kidnapping attempt, Fritz knew he needed to disappear for a while. He thought there was a mole in his organization giving up the whereabouts of his family and associates. Fritz promptly moved his family out of their apartment. He told everyone important to his operation to stay off 112th and lie low. That meant no beefs that would bring the cops sniffing around and possibly blow Fritz's cover. He temporarily relocated to an undisclosed location outside of the city, taking with him Ace, Hen Dog, and Fat E. It became clear that there were few people he could trust.

The four men stayed at the secret location for three months; during this time Fritz personally monitored all their calls. The only person Fritz allowed to travel into the city was Ace, who had to drive back and forth to court on a drug case that was eventually dropped.

Fritz was very shrewd and was able to flex his power even from the safe house, miles away from the block. He used his many resources and found his mole, the person he believed Steven Palmer, leader of Wild Cowboys, had planted on 112th Street. It turns out the man was from 112th, a cat named Russell "Sticks" Williams. Sticks thought he would be safe, figuring it was just a few addresses he would give, and following people around here and there. But in the end, Sticks paid for his betrayal with his life. It turned out, he was shot and killed a few weeks after the incident. He was into a lot of shady dealings, and would sell his momma out for a few bucks, so no one knows who shot and killed him. What became clear, is that his actions caught up with him.

---

[62] UNITED STATES of America, Appellee, v. Robert AULICINO, Jr., David Cleary, and Louis Ruggiero, Jr., Defendants-Appellants. (1995) Nos. 175, 176 and 641, Dockets 93-1883, 94-1027 and 94-1214. Retrieved from https://caselaw.findlaw.com/us-2nd-circuit/1432502.html.

CHAPTER EIGHTEEN

The Domino Effect Of The Game

IN THE DRUG GAME, THERE were rarely happy endings; prison, loss, and/ or death were almost inevitable. Very few got out the game unscathed, including a player's loved ones. Fritz always told his associates, you have to be smart to win at the game. There were people that didn't heed his warnings and had to learn the hard way.

Christopher Clemente, Hen Dog's brother, was a 19-year-old sophomore at the prestigious Wharton School of Business at the University of Pennsylvania. When he was home from school he'd helped his family with their neighborhood businesses. One day in January, Christopher decided to visit his brother at one of Fritz's many stash houses at 109.

Leah Bundy, at 21, was the mother of three children, ages 1, 2, and 3, respectively. Leah had also been in the stash house apartment visiting Hen Dog, whom she was seeing at the time. Hen Dog stepped out for some business, and Leah decided to hang out with Christopher and wait for him to return. It would be a decision she'd regret for the rest of her life.

On the night Christopher and Leah were waiting for Hen Dog in apartment 48, cops were responding to a radio call reporting a man shot in apartment 49, next door. The cops knocked on 49, but there was no answer.

"Who is it?" Christopher called out from behind the front door. The cops were so noisy, he mistakenly thought they were knocking on his door.

"The police. Open the door."

Christopher panicked. Leaving Leah in the back bedroom, he hurried around the apartment gathering all the drugs and guns he could find. He broke a window to get it open and cut his hand as he quickly tossed out a loaded Glock handgun, bags containing nearly 2,000 crack-filled vials, and a scale used to weigh drugs.

The cops heard the commotion as Christopher ran through the apartment and split up to investigate when they heard glass breaking. Some headed to the roof and some to the alley, where they found the various items tossed from apartment 48.

When Christopher thought he had gotten rid of all the visible drug paraphernalia—unaware that he was bleeding heavily—he allowed the cops to enter and search the premises for a person they believed he'd shot. The apartment was dimly lit, bare, and didn't look lived-in, which added to the police officers' curiosity. The only furnished room in the apartment was one of the two back bedrooms. They found Leah in one and asked if she lived there.

"Yes. Get the fuck out," Leah said immediately. They told her they would leave once they were done.

One cop inspected the bedroom in search of a gunshot victim or any signs of foul play. Instead he found more than 200 vials in a clear plastic bag on the floor and over $10,000, in mostly small bills, in plain sight on a night table. In a second unfurnished bedroom, they found a window security gate bent and stained with blood. Then they disco-vered a treasure chest of overlooked paraphernalia: a loaded gun, a bulletproof vest, a gun holster, a bag of ammunition, and a photograph of Leah with "Leah B. being a bitch" written across the bottom. The background of the picture showed the similar wall and mattress—it was the same room she was in and proved she had been in the apartment before.

In a hall closet in the apartment the cops found quantities of cocaine, beepers, vials, more cash, several items bearing his brother's name, and a ledger with Christopher's name on it. Leah and Christopher were both arrested.

Fritz learned about the arrests and was livid with Hen Dog. He'd tried to teach him how to play the game, get his money, and stay under the radar to avoid the cops. Hen Dog, who was married, liked using the apartment for his rendezvous with other women, which got Leah caught up. It was bad business and silly to have a drug ledger and mail in the apartment with the same names of individuals involved with that business. Fritz wanted to help Christopher and Leah, but it was Hen Dog's problem, and he needed to step up and fix it.

In court, the prosecutor found and released a picture of Christopher holding a variety of weapons to convince the court he wasn't just an innocent schoolboy.[63] Leah had a youthful offender misdemeanor drug conviction from 1986, when she'd tried to smuggle drugs to her mother at Rikers. She had a separate drug possession charge and a bench warrant too, which made her defense difficult. Prosecutors offered Leah and Christopher a plea

---

63   Sullivan, Ronald. "Former College Student Sentenced in Drug Case." The New York Times Archives, 27 February 1991, Section B, Page 2, https://www.nytimes.com/1991/02/27/nyregion/ former-college-student-sentenced-in-drug-case.html.

agreement of one-to-three years in prison. But when Christopher refused to accept the offer, Leah lost hers as well. In court, it didn't matter that Christopher was a former starting football lineman on an Ivy League scholarship, or that Leah had three children she'd leave behind if convicted.

Christopher and Leah were in the apartment with drugs, drug paraphernalia, and guns on their own accord, without coercion or force. Christopher claimed throughout the trial that the drugs in the apartment belonged to his brother, but the judge wouldn't hear it. Under the harsh drug laws, coined "Rockefeller Drug Laws," both were sentenced to a minimum of 15 years.

Leah were caught up in the wrong place at the wrong time.[64] She was eventually granted clemency by Governor George Pataki, but not before wasting 10 years behind bars. She was convicted on the strength of a single photo. While she was in prison, two of her three children were placed in the foster care system, while she fought for visitation of the third. The domino effects of the game were devastating, regardless of how deep you were in it.

---

[64] The PEOPLE of the State of New York, Respondent, v. Leah BUNDY, Defendant-Appellant. (1997) https://caselaw. findlaw.com/ny-supreme-court-appellate-division/1149895. html

CHAPTER NINETEEN

A Turning Point

The first time Fritz started showing signs that he was gravely ill was in 1990. Evelyn had to take him to the hospital, because he had grown weak with a high fever, and was unable to stand. He was admitted to New York Hospital in downtown Manhattan. The doctors thought Fritz had histoplasmosis, a type of lung infection caused by inhaling spores found in soil and bird droppings. The doctors ran several tests and kept him under observation. They were concerned specifically about Fritz's immune system.

Fritz was in the hospital for two weeks, while Ace handled his business and never missed a day visiting him there. If he got there after visiting hours, he would find a way to sneak up to his room. The nurses eventually let Ace visit after hours once it became clear he was going to see Fritz no matter what.

Once he was discharged, Fritz seemed to recover and was doing well until a few months later. This time it happened at home while Ace was with him. Fritz suddenly started to have an unstoppable coughing spell, followed by shortness of breath and chest pain. Ace took him to the hospital. He was admitted to Beth Israel Medical Center for a few days and quickly lost a significant amount of weight. His eyes became sunken with dark circles and he had uncontrollable tremors.

Fritz's inner circle didn't treat him any differently, but they knew he wasn't well. His mental and physical state changed dramatically over the past year; he was no longer the Fritz they knew. He had always been strong and steely, a man that took charge even in the most difficult of situations. Despite any condition Fritz may have been in, people looked to him for instruction, direction, and leadership—and they weren't seeing the same leadership anymore.

Fritz then began to display odd behavior, like wearing oversized coats on warm days and wasting money frivolously. It was out of character for him. When he was too weak to get out of bed, he conducted business from home. Fritz also started having intimate conversations with his crew about keeping emergency stashes for a rainy day. He had two large Pampers diaper boxes prepared to be sent to Sheila and Evelyn should things get too difficult. Little did he know those boxes would never reach them.

Meanwhile news about Fritz's illness was spreading on the streets. It wasn't something he could hide much longer. Charles, Chucky's son, was driving on 131st Street and Fifth Avenue when he saw his father sitting on the mailbox crying. He had never seen his father cry before. "They said Fritz dying from AIDS," Chucky explained. "I know that shit not true. They lying."

Chucky wasn't concerned about Fritz having AIDS, because he figured Fritz had enough money to find the best doctors and a cure. He was more upset about losing someone who had been a brother to him. Chucky did all that he could to care for Fritz, standing by his side until a turn of events altered the course of his and Ace's lives forever.

1991 was a turning point in Harlem, in Fritz's life, and in his family's life. No one was prepared for what came next. Things started to change quickly, one after another. A seemingly endless and relentless turn of events changed their lives, and when the dust settled, nothing would be the same again.

The beginning of the end started three years earlier, in November 1988. On 117th Street and Madison Avenue, not far from where Ace lived, the body of a cab driver, Miguel Antonio Terrero, was found dead. He'd been shot twice but no weapons were recovered at the scene and no arrest made at the time.

The next day, Officer Orlando Rosario of the 25th Precinct was assigned to patrol 115th–121st Street, Lexington Avenue to Fifth Avenue. A Hispanic man approached Rosario and told him about a bullet shell in the street. Officer Rosario found the shell casing from a .380 automatic about 260 feet from where Terrero's body had been found. Several cops had already closely combed the crime scene for hours the day before and came up with nothing. Was it a stroke of luck or an unlikely coincidence that Officer Rosario ran into a concerned citizen looking to do his civic duty?

A month after Terrero's murder, on December 20, the 25th received an anonymous tip that a witness saw a man shoot Miguel Antonio Terrero. The alleged eyewitness, a crackhead, prostitute, and a familiar face at the 25th Precinct—Zenola Samantha Lewis—walked in and gave her statement. Lewis viewed photographs and recognized an old mugshot of Ace at 18 years old, taken after a false arrest back on August 16, 1985, which should have been destroyed. Lewis identified Ace as Terrero's shooter and gave a statement to the police.

According to Lewis, she was hanging out in the kitchen with Hector Osorio at 61 East 117th Street the night of the shooting. While Hector smoked crack, Lewis watched two men arguing outside the window on a dimly lit street. She claimed she saw Ace shoot Terrero, pass the gun to another man, and take an envelope out of Terrero's jacket.

Lewis further claimed that when she left Hector's apartment, she saw Ace standing in the crowd watching as the cops interviewed possible witnesses nearby. Lewis called an acquaintance, Detective Bobby Stewart, at the 25th Precinct a few minutes after witnessing the murder and reported the shooting. Detective Stewart took Lewis's statement, but wouldn't report it for another month.

Several days later, unknown to Ace, his name was put on an arrest warrant issued for the murder of Miguel Antonio Terrero.

Fast forward almost three years later. On February 13, 1991, Ace was on the corner of 129th Street and Madison Avenue chatting openly and casually with his brother and two friends. Suddenly an unmarked police vehicle appeared. A detective approached and showed Ace the old photo of himself the police had shown Zenola Lewis.

"Is that you?" the detective asked. "Yes," Ace responded, unconcerned.

"You're under arrest," the detective said, as his partner joined him.

The first detective proceeded to read Ace his Miranda rights and pat him down, while the second pulled out his handcuffs to arrest him. Ace refused to allow the handcuffing and agreed to go to the precinct without incident. He was shocked to find out he was being charged with the murder of a man he'd never met or known three years ago.

Ace had the best lawyers fighting his case. He didn't know the victim or the witness and wasn't worried, because he felt he was obviously innocent of all charges in this murder case. But he overestimated the jury, who saw things differently. Ace was found guilty on four counts, including murder in the second degree. In March 1992, Ace was sentenced to twenty years to life.[65]

A few months after, Officer Rosario was arrested with three other officers in the 25th for numerous felony charges, including bribery, coercion, unlawful imprisonment, and official misconduct.[66] Ace believed Rosario set him up for Miguel Antonio Terrero's murder as well.

Ace's sentencing was devastating news for Fritz. He was losing not only a lieutenant, but a true brother and friend. Chucky was the only other person Fritz could trust, but he wasn't a drug dealer. Chucky was content with coaching his youth basketball team in the Kingdome Classics on 115th and Lenox in Harlem. Chucky was also happy managing Martin's Game Room when he wasn't working his regular 9 to 5, as well as protecting Fritz from anyone who would try to take advantage of or cross him. Chucky was quiet, well mannered, and not to be messed with, everyone knew that. With Ace in jail and Chucky more of an enforcer than a drug dealer, Fritz had no other choice but to rely on those he knew but did not necessarily trust to help run his business.

Three months after Ace went to jail, Fritz was struck another devastating blow. One Sunday in May 1991, according to Shelagh,

---

[65] The PEOPLE of the State of New York, Respondent, v. Adrian SMALL, Defendant. (1991) (see Brief Case Summary Pg 205)

[66] Supreme Court, Appellate Division, First Department, New York. The PEOPLE of the State of New York, Respondent, v. Patricia FEERICK, Defendant-Appellant. The PEOPLE of the State of New York, Respondent, v. Mayra SCHULTZ, Defendant-Appellant. The PEOPLE of the State of New York, Respondent, v. John DeVITO, Defendant-Appellant. The PEOPLE of the State of New York, Respondent, v. Orlando ROSARIO (The Officer that arrested Ace), Defendant-Appellant. (1998) https://caselaw.findlaw.com/ny-supreme-court-appellate-division/1419959.html.

Chucky left their Harlem apartment at 109 and headed to the Bronx. Chucky was living in the Patterson Houses in the Bronx with his new wife, Maddy, and their two children. It wasn't quite clear at that time that Chucky was married to Maddy, but it was evident that their relation was serious, and they had two children together. However, Shelagh believed he was leaving Maddy and coming back home to her and their three children. Shelagh and Chucky were together for many years throughout his infidelities. He would leave but always find himself back on her doorstep. She figured the same would happen this time.

One day out of the blue, Chucky asked Shelagh if he could take their son Malik down south with him, offering no further explanation.

"Hell no!" Shelagh responded.

Chucky left without him and returned to New York a few weeks later wearing a wedding band. He told Shelagh he had married Maddy. She was heartbroken until he came back knocking on her door a few months later. He wanted back in. Things weren't working out with his new wife.

As she had numerous times before, Shelagh forgave Chucky and let him back in. At first Chucky went back and forth between the two households, trying to please both women and care for his children with them as well as the children he had outside of both their relationships. Chucky had a hard time being with only one woman—he was a true rolling stone. He loved women and the children he fathered with them, and he took care of them as best he could, even if he couldn't commit to one family. Tensions between both women came to a head when Maddy came banging on Shelagh's door one night looking for him.

Shelagh opened the door. "What do you want? Your man is in my bed sleep. If you don't get away from my door, I'ma let these dogs loose," she said.

Chucky knew both women were at their breaking point. He had been bouncing from spot to spot, and it proved unmanageable. Ultimately, Chucky decided he and Shelagh had too much history to throw away despite his many mistakes. They had been together long before all the money and women, before Fritz had created a drug empire. Chucky wanted to work things out with her. He stayed put that night but went up to the Bronx to get his things from Maddy.

That spring night in May was warm, and Shelagh sat outside 109 with their children and waited for her man to come back. It was her birthday the next day and she was looking forward to rekindling things with a romantic night. The minutes crept by. She sent her kids to bed. Midnight came and Shelagh was still on the stoop at 109 waiting on Chucky. He never made it back to her.

In the meantime, Chucky's son Charles—whom he had groomed to help with Fritz's business, and was said to be humble like his father, but lethal if he had to be lethal—got a call from Maddy in the wee hours of the morning.

"Have you seen your father?" Maddy said.

Charles had seen his father earlier that day and knew that he hadn't planned on going home to Maddy that night; Charles didn't want to say the wrong thing, in case his father was with another woman and had used him as an alibi.

"Yeah, I was just with him," Charles answered.

"Well, somebody just shot him," Maddy replied.

Charles hung up in disbelief. He and his sister hurried over to Patterson Houses, where Maddy lived. They arrived and saw cops swarming the area. The entire block was taped off with yellow caution tape, and in the center of it all was a body. Charles didn't believe it was his father. He pushed past the officers, and under the yellow caution tape. Charles saw Chucky's body, covered in blood and riddled with bullet holes. He stared into his father's eyes that were still open. It couldn't be.

They left the scene to find Shelagh, who they found on the stoop at 1:30 AM still waiting for Chucky. Charles jumped out of the car, hysterical, and screaming, "Shelagh, Shelagh, Daddy's dead, Daddy's dead!"

Who had Chucky murdered? The rumors spread fast through Harlem and the Bronx. Was it about one of his baby mamas? Did someone want him out of the way to get to Fritz? Was it jealousy? Did a rival eliminate Ace and Chucky, his top two guys, in hopes to cripple his business? There were a lot of unanswered questions.

The streets knew the truth, but no one was talking. It was clearly a setup. Chucky had been followed, or the hitmen knew he'd be visiting Maddy that day in the Patterson Houses. They knew what his car looked like and waited until he drove up in his blue Suburban truck.

Chucky was getting out of the truck when he was ambushed by two men. There was a struggle and Chucky fought back, but ultimately, he was shot several times in the chest and once in the head.[67]

Tragedy and grief lingered. When Fritz found out that Chucky was killed, he was overcome with grief, so much so he couldn't attend Chucky's funeral. He did not want his last memory of Chucky to be of him in a casket. His death affected many people very deeply. It took a toll on Fritz, the women in Chucky's life,

---

[67]   (56b) Hevesi, Dennis. "9 Men Posing as Police Are Indicted in 3 Murders." The New York Times Archives, 30 September 1992, Section B, Page 3, https://www.nytimes.com/1992/09/30/nyregion/9-men-posing-as-police-are-indicted-in-3-murders.html.

and the children he had with them. It also affected all the young men and women he mentored.

Chucky's brother Eddie became the father figure to the 17 children he'd left behind, and Fritz the financial benefactor. Shelagh, his first love and high school sweetheart, was inconsolable. She blamed herself for sending Chucky back to the Bronx to get his things. Maybe if he hadn't left he would still be alive. She also blamed Maddy for coming between them, knowing Chucky had a family. Maybe if he hadn't got involved with Maddy he'd still be alive.

Shelagh wanted revenge but couldn't chance leaving her family if she was arrested. So, after Chucky's funeral, with only the clothes on her back, she left it all behind: the money, the arsenal of guns, the drugs, the jewelry, the cars, everything. She left her children in the care of her family, and left town determined never to return to that life.

CHAPTER TWENTY

Running Out Of Time

THE SANDS IN THE HOURGLASS of time were running out for Fritz. The end was near. Fritz knew it, and so did his immediate family, his inner circle, and the vultures that gathered to feed on the carrion.

Ace was gone, in jail serving a 20-year sentence. Chucky was dead. The two most important men in his life were no longer with him. Fritz was getting sicker and he seemed to stop caring about life and himself. He was still making money and his empire was growing, but this had never ever fazed him, and without Ace and Chucky, it was even less of a concern. There was no one he could trust like he trusted those men.

When making money wasn't exciting anymore, Fritz started giving it away. People on 112th Street thought Fritz's illness was affecting his brain, because he would routinely throw thousands of dollars out of his apartment window. The truth was, he knew his fate. He gave the money away because he could, and he had so much of it. Fritz knew he couldn't take it with him.

JD and Hen Dog knew where all Fritz's money and drugs were stashed. They were the only two left with keys to Fritz's apartments. They never returned the keys to his sister, who lived in the building right next door. They had access to millions of dollars and they helped themselves. They splurged, indulged, and lived like ballers on Fritz's money.

Hen Dog would often come to Ace's trial in a fur coat, wearing big diamond stud earrings and tons of flashy jewelry, looking like Mr. T from *The A-Team*.[68] While in jail, Ace heard how Hen Dog was putting up girls in houses and buying cars and motorcycles. While Ace was fighting for his freedom and Fritz for his life, these guys were having a party like everything was good. Ace knew Hen Dog never made enough money to afford the lifestyle he was now living, but he played it cool, keeping his eyes and ears open.

Ace would speak with JD from behind the prison walls. JD was having problems in the streets collecting Fritz's money, now that Fritz was sick and unable to manage his affairs. Dudes on the streets didn't respect JD the way they did Fritz. Many thought JD was soft and got lucky connecting with Fritz. The word on the streets was Fritz was dying. Fritz's enforcer Chucky was dead and his right-hand Ace was doing a long bid, so paying JD what they owed Fritz wasn't something many was willing to do.

"Dudes acting like they don't want to give up that money they owe Fritz," JD said. "I think they want to rock me, so they don't have to."

"Don't worry about that. Do what I need you to do and when I come home I'll handle that," Ace responded.

JD would talk to Ace about how Hen Dog was stealing, but Ace knew that Hen Dog wasn't the only one. JD was also getting his share of the pie. How else could he afford buying property down south? He had been expressing to Ace on visits of this

---

[68] The A-Team, Created by Frank Lupo, Stephen J. Cannell, NBC Universal Television, 1983–1987. TV Series

so-called investment into real estate in the Carolina's and had now been boldly explaining to Ace how he planned to rent the apartments out to students at the nearby college. Ace let him talk, as his main focus at the time was his freedom and he needed JD's help for that. JD had access to his money in the stash house.

Ace needed to keep the peace for now. He needed to make sure his criminal defense team on his murder case from 1988 got paid. Ace also needed JD to contact his attorneys and the private investigator on his case, because he had information on the eyewitness, Zenola Samantha Lewis, that would prove she was lying and that he was innocent.

"My people be seeing the witness. They know where she live," Ace told JD. "All I need you to do is get the private investigator and lawyer to go see her…that's it…I don't need nobody to approach her. I don't want her to make up no lies, no stories, just to tell the truth… and ask why she saying it was me? That's all I need you to do, let them handle it. All I need her to do is tell the truth."

"Don't worry about it. I got you," JD responded.

However, JD didn't have any plans to help Ace. Like Ace, JD wanted him to think they were all good. The truth was JD played Ace close, accepted his calls, and even visited him because he needed to know if and when he was coming home. JD had resented Ace from day one and never got over Fritz bringing Ace into his inner circle over him.

JD wanted to be the boss, wanted control over the connect, and had no plans to help Ace get out. Subsequently, Ace was found guilty for the murder of Miguel Antonio Terrero in 1992. Ace never heard from JD again.

Back before JD and Hen Dog began their quest of stealing from Fritz, Ace remembered when Fritz initially told him to give JD and Hen Dog keys to the stash house. Ace was reluctant, almost seeing into the future. Still, he did as he was told and trusted Fritz. JD and Hen Dog needed access to pick up and drop off money, while Ace was responsible for everything else pertaining to the connect and distribution. Deep down though, JD and Hen Dog were jealous of both men. When Fritz fell ill, they took advantage of the situation and seized the opportunity. They both failed miserably.

Ace was always a stand-up guy who lived by the code of the streets. Although JD and others turned their back on him and left him in jail to rot, Ace never rolled over, he never sacrificed his principles by snitching to gain his freedom or shorten his time. Was Ace angry? Of course he was. It took Ace years to let go and not be so angry, about Fritz's treatment, about not being able to say goodbye to Chucky. The only person who was able to help him through the pain and anger was his mother. The only thing on his mind was killing. Ace wanted revenge on all the people who did wrong by Fritz at a critical time during his illness.

Lauren, the mother of one of Fritz's sons, became Fritz's caretaker, and Peggy, his long-time confidante and assistant, also helped care for him. After a few weeks passed, Evelyn grew concerned because she hadn't heard from her brother. She called the house several times, but Lauren refused to give Fritz the phone. "Fritz isn't feeling well today," was always her excuse.

Evelyn went to the apartment on several occasions and knocked on the door, but there was never any answer. Worried, Evelyn reached out to their mother in South Carolina to fill her in. A few weeks later Mama Simmons came up to New York and they went together to Lauren's apartment. Lauren finally opened the door and let them in.

When Evelyn and Mama Simmons saw Fritz they were horrified by his skeletal appearance. He was emaciated and weak, barely hanging on. They removed Fritz from the apartment and took him down south to care for him.

The last time Ace heard Fritz's voice he cried over the phone. Fritz was too weak to visit him, so a brief phone conversation was set up with Ace from prison.

"I miss you, man," Fritz said.

Fritz cried so much he could barely talk to Ace, so he handed the phone to JD, who was with him. Ace had never heard Fritz cry, so the sound of his voice cracking stayed with him. Ace believed those around him could have done more. Ace once again hoped JD would do right by Fritz and pleaded with him to make sure Fritz got to the hospital before hanging up the phone that day, but true to form JD didn't keep his word.

Fritz's unexpected illness and departure down south created a power struggle. No one knew who was in control with Fritz out of commission. Was it JD or Hen Dog? Fritz didn't put either one in charge, but they were the only ones left with keys to the stash houses and close ties to Fritz.

Unfortunately, their greed and unwillingness to work as a team would be their downfall. Their scheming and making moves behind the other's back with Fritz's drugs and money exposed the problems in Fritz's camp. The streets went into panic mode. Who were they going to get their drugs from now, and at what price?

Chucky and Ace were the only people privy to the ins and outs of Fritz's business and they were gone. No one except Fritz knew what the next man was doing and who owed what. This business tactic protected the family and anyone making money with Fritz, but it also made it difficult to decipher what he had, who could be trusted with it, and who his partners were.

Rival crews went into a frenzy. Bodies piled up on the streets of Harlem, as those who owed Fritz refused to pay. They figured a dead man couldn't collect on a debt. Rumor was, a known drug dealer in Harlem named Allen Lord owed Fritz money. Hen Dog saw Allen at car wash at 148th Street on Amsterdam.

He approached him and words were exchanged. Then Hen Dog pulled out a gun and killed him, though Fritz hadn't ordered Allen's hit or anyone else's.

The streets weren't the only ones concerned about Fritz's whereabouts and his business. Fritz had never been late with a payment to the Medellín Cartel, nor the monthly 300-500 kilos of cocaine he picked up in the Bronx. There were kilos of the cartel's cocaine and over $6 million in Fritz's apartment at 109 before Fritz and Ace went on hiatus. The debt owed to the cartel was $3 million plus, which was given to a cartel associate by JD.

The Medellín Cartel didn't care about the money Fritz owed, because he had made them millions in the past. What they did care about were the streets whispering about Fritz dying of AIDS, and that he had run off with the cartel's money. The rumors disrespected the cartel. They sent an associate to Harlem for answers and found JD. JD informed the cartel associate where to find Fritz and struck up a side deal to keep moving their drugs while Fritz and Ace were out of commission.

By now, Fritz had to be hospitalized. He was on a respirator, barely breathing, and semi-conscious. Evelyn was visiting with Fritz when a well-dressed Hispanic man walked into the hospital room.

"Who are you?" Evelyn asked.

"A friend. My associates and I were doing business with Fritz. We heard he was sick and I needed to see for myself," he said.

"Well you see he's very sick and not going nowhere anytime soon," Evelyn responded.

"Yes, I see. I just want you to know that we will not be bothering your family again. I wish him a speedy recovery. Take care," he said and left.

As Fritz lay in his hospital room in his final days, many dirty deeds came to light. One day his sister Evelyn and niece Sandra were visiting when Sandra's cell phone rang. When she answered she heard an unfamiliar male voice. He told her that he had been with Lauren at a hotel and wanted to return the wallet she had left behind. It infuriated Evelyn and confirmed her suspicions that Lauren had been cheating while Fritz fought for his life.

Fritz had fought many battles in the street, but this was one fight he could not win. The day finally came when the doctor informed the family that there was no more that they could do for him. His illness had become terminal and the doctor was baffled over it. After various tests and blood work, the doctor determined that an unknown substance found in Fritz's system, possibly a poison, was killing him. It wasn't the AIDS virus many still believe today, but a poison that lead to his rapid deterioration and death.

Fritz's illness took a particularly hard toll on Sheila. She was already in counseling and dealing with her demons: the repeated rapes by her stepfather, the death of her son, the murder of her mother, and now the inevitable death of her brother. It was too much for her to handle. The drugs her brother had given her to become self-sufficient became her vice. But after a while even that was no longer an escape. Ultimately, she had a nervous breakdown and had to be hospitalized. Evelyn said the skies were clear and the sun shined bright when Fritz crossed over. When Evelyn and her daughter came to visit him, there was a sense of calm and peacefulness in the room. She noticed the rays of sunlight seemed to surround Fritz. Evelyn knew something wondrous was happening but didn't realize she was seeing her brother for the last time.

On Friday, August 16, 1991, two months after Chucky's murder, Fritz crossed over. His death wasn't a tragedy to his family in the typical sense. He wasn't shot down in the streets, and he had spent his last days surrounded by the love of his family. Fritz was a man of integrity and courage, and despite his profession, he lived a life of generosity and social consciousness. He lived a hard life on the streets and abided by its rules, but he gave back to his community and was loved for it. Although many tried, there would never be another like him.

CHAPTER TWENTY ONE

The End

*Hear counsel, and receive instruction,
that thy may be wise in thy latter end.*

—PROVERBS 19:20

People got grimy after Fritz passed. There was no one responsible left to oversee or manage the drugs and money left behind. People thought Fritz left large sums of money with his sister, Evelyn. One night, very late there was a knock-on Evelyn's door.

"Who is it?" Evelyn asked.

"JD sent us upstairs to use the phone," a man said.

Evelyn peeked out the peephole. Two men stood outside her door. She had never seen them before in her life. *There were plenty of pay phones on the street, why knock on my door?* she thought. She was a working woman and not from the street, but her mama didn't raise no fool. She quietly moved away from the door and sat down. The men knocked a few more times. She then heard them walk away and the elevator door slide open and close. She hurried to the window and saw them walk up the street and disappear into the darkness.

Fritz used to be Harlem's cocaine consignment king—if you mentioned 112th Street in Harlem, everyone knew who ran that block and the love the block had for Fritz. And yet it's been over three decades since Fritz passed, and there has not been one mural or a cookout in his memory.

"Santa Claus gone, ain't no more got damn Santa Claus," Evelyn responded, when people began asking who'd play beneficiary to the neighborhood's needy. "That's over. Fritz tried to teach y'all how to help yourself…you didn't do it. It's no more."

Many thought Fritz's family should not be hurting for money. Fritz made millions on the streets several times over. Fritz left money for all of his people, including Evelyn and Sheila. It just never got to them.

Fritz left their money with a close family associate, Harry, a businessman in construction who provided jobs for a lot of guys in the neighborhood coming home from prison. Fritz had known Harry for quite some time and trusted him to take care of matters such as making sure his family would get money put away for them. Harry dated Fritz's cousin, Chrissy, and they had a child together—Fritz had known Harry way before that, and they remained very good friends even after the couple's breakup.

Fritz had requested that Harry hand-deliver the "rainy day" Pampers boxes of money to Evelyn and Sheila. They didn't find out until months after Fritz's death that Harry was meant to make that delivery. Sheila was shocked to learn from a family friend that Harry ran off with all of it. She would later find out he used the money on his wedding and bought a house down south for his wife and kids.

Fritz had always planned to get out the game and invest his money in real estate; Fritz and Ace talked about it all the time. Harlem was changing, and they had bigger plans for themselves beyond the drug game.

Fritz was the first to purchase a brownstone out of the two. He didn't have a regular 9 to 5 at the time and couldn't show a source of income. Fritz didn't want the extra attention or be under the Fed's radar, so purchasing expensive items in a trusted family members' name kept the Feds at bay. He purchased a corner brownstone on Lenox Avenue, now Malcolm X Boulevard, with an in-law, Sylvia. He trusted Sylvia and left his name off of the deed, placing the brownstone in her name. Fritz shared the property, used the brownstone for collateral to pay the $10,000-$15,000 bail for his workers when they got busted. He also stashed large sums of money and bagged drugs in one of the rooms.

There was an abandoned brownstone next door that Ace had been checking out. The owner of the property was looking to sell for $75,000. Ace was in negotiation with the owner when he was arrested in 1991. Ace asked Fritz to handle things, and Fritz passed this responsibility to Sylvia, which legitimized it. Sylvia negotiated a payment plan for purchasing Ace's brownstone. Fritz had given Sylvia $50,000 in cash of Ace's money as a down payment to the owner. Soon after, however, Fritz would succumb to his illness and Ace's brownstone would be sold for a high profit, but not by Ace.

Ace learned a lot about real estate while incarcerated and taught a training course to other inmates. He sent his and Evelyn's mother, Joyce, to the brownstone to speak with Sylvia, not knowing the home had been sold from under him. Sylvia told Evelyn and Joyce point blank that she'd never received any money for the brownstone from Fritz and had bought it herself. She went on that she could no longer afford to pay the taxes on the property and let it go. Sylvia knew where Evelyn and other relatives of Ace's lived. It wasn't Sylvia's to sell, but she did, because she could. Greed managed to disrupt even this tight-knit family. The streets rumored that Sylvia had even set Ace up. After Fritz passed, it would benefit Sylvia if Ace was also out of the picture.

As of this book's publishing, Sylvia still owns the Lenox Avenue brownstone. She rents space out for special events and to politicians to use as a campaign office during elections. She recently made a deal with producers at Netflix to shoot a popular series on the Harlem property. One of the characters in the show was even named Fritz, although the family did not consent, no papers were sign or agreements made, and no check was ever written to the family to use Fritz likeness or a character that resembled Fritz's lifestyle.

To add insult to injury, a handful of individuals close to the family wanted Fritz's body brought back to New York for a funeral service for his friends who couldn't make it to the service down south. But they were either unwilling or thought it was the family's responsibility to pay the expense to transport Fritz's body. Many bragged how they helped with his burial, how they paid for buses to take people from New York to South Carolina and to put them up in hotels. But wasn't that the least they could do, with all the money stashes Fritz and Ace left behind?

Evelyn never forgave anyone who betrayed their family once Fritz was dead. They had treated him as their personal cash cow. Sheila, though, forgave those who didn't know any better.

There are still people who gossip idly on the street and believe just because someone lived or hung out on 112th Street that he's knowledgeable about all things Fritz. People tend to also mention Hen Dog's and JD's names along with Fritz's. Sheila's advice to them: Don't do it; neither one is worthy of that honor.

Right after Fritz passed JD dropped by Evelyn's to visit and say he felt lost and confused since Fritz's death; he needed to hang out in his room, feel his presence. That was where he also broke down on his knees and cried.

"Fritz I miss you. What I'ma do now Fritz," JD wailed.

Evelyn wouldn't see JD again until he came knocking on the door to borrow some money to bail out Albee, a former worker of JD's. Evelyn understood the transaction to be a loan. Evelyn would later see Albee on the street and find out that he had not even been arrested. It would be the last time Evelyn would see her money or JD again. True to form, he had manipulated and used Evelyn for his own gain.

As for Hen Dog, he had always been trigger happy and reckless, in love with the gangster life, never able to be low-key. In the end it brought him down.

In 1992, the apartment Hen Dog and his girlfriend shared was robbed. Hen Dog wasn't home during the robbery but his girlfriend was, and she was shot and wounded. Hen Dog was told that a neighborhood guy named Po, a gun runner, had something to do with the robbery. Hen Dog and a few of his crew approached Po about the incident. Po showed him his release papers, proving that he was in jail at the time. Hen Dog was so angry that he refused to believe him. Hen Dog and his friends beat up Po in the street, then Hen Dog chased Po through the Soundview projects at gunpoint.

After that, Hen Dog harassed Po every time he had the chance. Po couldn't get a break—even when he was with his mother, Hen Dog would disrespect him, pulling out his gun and threatening him.

Hen Dog knew deep down that Po had nothing to do with the robbery. But he was a bully, a showboat who got his kicks putting fear into people. Po just wanted to be left alone, but he knew that it wasn't an option. Po left New York and went down south for a while, hoping that when he returned things would cool down, but they didn't. Hen Dog continued to harass him whenever he saw him. What Hen Dog didn't know was that when Po returned to the Bronx, he brought back a gun.

On May 14, 1992, Hen Dog was exiting a restaurant when he saw Po. At first he was surprised that he was walking toward him and not running the other way as usual. That's when Hen Dog saw a gun in Po's hand and tried to run. Po knew that Hen Dog wore a bulletproof vest and shot him in his leg, which knocked Hen Dog to the ground. Po stood over him.

"Say sorry," Po said.

"Fuck you!" Hen Dog yelled at him.

"Say sorry," Po said repeatedly. He wasn't a killer. He didn't want to kill him.

"Fuck you!" Hen Dog repeated.

Even with one bullet already in his leg and Po pointing his gun at him with his finger on the trigger, Hen Dog still refused to apologize. Maybe he thought it was cool or gangster to go out in blaze of glory. But there was no glory. Po pulled the trigger, killed him, then immediately turned himself in to the police.

As for JD, karma would catch up with him as well. Soon after Hen Dog's murder, JD was arrested for drug possession and received a 10-year-to-life sentence in a federal prison.

EPILOGUE

Do You Remember Me, Harlem? Be careful that you do not forget the LORD, who brought you out of Egypt, out of the land of Slavery.

—DEUTERONOMY 6:12

WITHOUT FRITZ IN CHARGE, THERE was no structure to drug dealing in the neighborhood, and mistakes were made that attracted the attention of the nearby 28th Precinct. Officers also noticed young people on 112th Street wearing the logo "No Fear" on their hats or T-shirts. What they couldn't know was that it was a way for neighborhood folks to pay homage to Fritz and others who had died. This is how local guys were mistakenly labeled by the cops as part of the 112th Street "No Fear Gang." According to a *New York Times* piece, the No Fear Gang began selling crack and heroin in the neighborhood in the 1980s, terrorizing rival dealers and gaining a hold on the territory along St. Nicholas Avenue just north of Central

Park.[69] They estimated that the gang cleared three million a year before the police began tracking them. After that, the amount mysteriously dropped to $500,000, as if no one really knew what they were talking about. Quite frankly, they didn't. There was never a "No Fear Gang", as some wanted people to think. The decrease in any money the block was raking in, was because Fritz was gone. The police were clueless and never knew that Fritz was the man in 112th Street that ran a multimillion-dollar drug operation.

THE PRESENCE OF 28TH PRECINCT vans on street corners have kept dealers at bay. Harlem is now called New Harlem. Gentrification is on the rise; the demographics are changing, and Black folks are becoming the minority. The pricey luxury condominiums being built are too steep for the pockets of many long-time Harlemites. Mom-and-pop stores and family-run restaurants are being pushed out or sold to the highest bidder to make room for big corporate franchises. On a hot summer night along 8th Avenue/Frederick Douglass Boulevard, now called Restaurant Row, you'll find many people sitting outside eating at the sidewalk cafes, mostly white folks. Harlem was once known for its ballers, gangsters, kingpins, fashion, and urban nightlife, but those days are long gone. Harlem will never be the same.

There are no more handouts and no more consignment street

---

[69] Siemaszko, Corky and Ross, Barbara. "31 Nabbed In Drug-Gang Bust." New York Daily News, 8 November 1996, https://www.nydailynews.com/archives/news/31-nabbed-drug-gang-bust-article-1.737351.

dealing, it's cash and carry only, if you can find someone to trust you enough to get it. The money is not the same. The people are not the same. Snitching and hating on the next man is the norm and at an all-time high. It's every man for himself, so remember to watch your back. There are no more loyal soldiers. Fritz unified many in the community, even if his ways and means were not always lawful. In the end, Fritz wanted to take care of his friends and family, and he did his best to do that.

Today most people won't discuss Fritz; they don't want their dirty laundry aired about why Fritz curbed them. They don't want to admit they smoked the crack instead of selling it, or that they mismanaged money, or made backdoor deals. Nowadays, the only acknowledgment Fritz gets outside of his immediate family is from Big Gee, Ace, Darryl, Chucky's son, Charles, and strangers on social media. But rest assured, from the 1980s up until his death in 1991, 112th Street was run by Richard "Fritz" Simmons. He was a one-man syndicate, Harlem's King of Consignment.

A DAUGHTER'S LOVE LETTER

ERIN CUNNINGHAM

Richard "Fritz" Simmons' Daughter
CEO of ReBourne NYC

Dear Dad,

Don't even really know where to begin. I wish you were here so I'd could just touch you. I wish I could tell you everything you've missed but then I remind myself that you're watching us all. I'm grateful to know I'm apart of you. I feel you with me in all that I do. Aunt Evelyn says I act just like you. It's crazy how things are passed down right? Not a day goes by that I don't think about you or wonder what things would be like if you were still here. I daydream about all the things we never got to do together but I know I can't challenge why God took you from us. Maybe you were just too good for the world. A girl growing up without her father is rough, so many things I wish you could've saw me through. I know things would've been different had you been here. No worries though your name lives on and I have many stories to hold me over till we meet again. I'm honored to be a part of your legacy and one of your girls. I take pride in it, but I know you see that. I love you forever and ever dad.

Love,
Erin Your Baby Girl

SHEILA'S MESSAGE OF APPRECIATION

Richard "FRITZ" Simmons Half-Sister

First and foremost, I'd like to thank my higher power, God. You walked me through many life lessons and experiences, only to equate to one thing, a strong-willed woman. I always kept the faith that you'd see me through those dark times and now my days are bright.

To my family, particularly my grandparents and siblings, thank you all for rallying around and supporting my dreams and goals. It feels good to know that I have your love and encouragement. It makes it all worthwhile.

To my children, Nicole, Darryl, Jr. (R.I.P.), Neil, Raven, and Money, I love you guys and I hope you see me getting my hustle on, so that you can reap the rewards. Watch and learn, so that when the torch is passed to you, you can run this race and not get tired.

My husband, Russell Wallace, thank you for being patient, for understanding and loving me, and for wiping away my tears. I cry a lot at night and being the husband, you are I want to thank you for always being there. When I look back on all of our sweet moments and exciting adventures, the day-to-day challenges and accomplishments, I can't imagine anyone who would be a better partner and friend.

My big sister, Evelyn Simmons. I love you with everything I have. You were always there for me and the kids. I cherish all the moments we shared and the time we spend together.

My BFF, Tiffany Simone Fulton n/k/a Harlem Holiday you came into my life when I lost my grandma. We clicked from day one. We hit it off like peanut butter and jelly. Thank you for always being there. I can call on you any time of the day and you are there. I love you, sister girl. I want to also thank your moms, Mrs. Vergie M. Green-Harris (my adopted mother) and your son, Ronnie Love (my nephew), for accepting me into the family. Love you both.

Ace Small, so sorry you are not here, but you are just a phone call away. Love you li'l brother. Thanks for dropping the real facts. Kisses.

Darryl Davis, you know you are family. I remember on my birthday when you brought a cake and smashed it in my face. Always enjoyed my time with you. Love you to the moon and back.

First Corinthian Baptist Church (FCBC), Pastor Michael Warlord. I want to thank you for being a great teacher. I was falling apart when I came to FCBC. FCBC helped me learn how to deal with myself and my past. God is good, *all the time.* Thank you and the church family for the love you've shown me, it changed my life. Pastor Kendra, thank you for letting me open up in session with you. You showed me how to deal with my pain. *Thank you.*

Don Diva Magazine, Editor-in-Chief, Kevin Chiles, thank you for being there and publishing my brother's story. It meant a lot to my sister and me. Much love.

Thank you, Lamont Whealton, Ray Burgess, Reginald Wiggins aka Rambo, Freddy aka Trick, Kashmir Peterson, and Gums for sharing your insight about the book. Much love.

My two adopted grandmas, Mae Rose and Maggie, thank you for all your wise words and your wisdom. Love You Divas.

Sheila Coleman it has been a long time since I saw you. I will stay in touch from this day on. Much love diva.

My building, 480 8th Avenue and Riverdale family, much love.

ADRIAN "ACE" SMALL BRIEF CASE SUMMARY

Indictment No.: 1724-91 Trail Judge: Renee White

Defendant's Lawyers: Irvin Levine and Mel Sachs

Thursday, November 17, 1988 about approximately 10:45 PM, on 117th Street and Madison Avenue the body of a cab driver, MIGUEL ANTONIO TERRERO is robbed and found dead lying face down bleeding, with two bullet wounds.

Friday, November 18, 1988, Officer Orlando Rosario of the 25th Precinct is assigned to patrol 115th – 121st Street, Lexington Avenue to Fifth Avenue. While on foot patrol, a Hispanic man stated to Officer Rosario that he seen a bullet shell in the street and directed the officer to the bullet.

Tuesday, December 20, 1988, the 25th Precinct received an anonymous tip that a witness and a police informant, ZENOLA SAMANTHA LEWIS observed a man, pull out a gun and shoot Miguel Antonio Terrero. The witness identifies a man in the police book of mug shots.

Thursday, December 29, 1988, an arrest warrant is issued on ADRIAN "ACE" SMALL for the murder of Miguel Antonio Terrero.

Wednesday, September 26, 1990 OFFICER ORLANDO ROSARIO and three other officers in the 25th Precinct are charged with numerous felony charges, including bribery, coercion, unlawful imprisonment, and official misconduct.

Wednesday, February 13, 1991, Adrian Small is arrested for the murder of Miguel Antonio Terrero.

Friday, March 26, 1992, Adrian Small is found guilty on four counts; guilty of murder in the second degree, guilty of criminal use of a firearm in the first degree, guilty of criminal possession of a weapon in the second degree, and guilty of criminal possession of a weapon in the third degree. He is sentenced to twenty years to life.

Monday, December 23, 2013, Adrian Small is released, but an immigration hold status is placed while he is still in custody.

Tuesday, March 18, 2014, Adrian Small is deported, after serving 23 years, 1 month, and 5 days, in New York State prison systems, for a crime he still proclaims he is innocent of.

*Adrian "Ace" Small has tried to appeal his murder case, but his non-citizenship makes it hard to fight and get his case overturned overseas. Ace is restricted from returning to the U.S. and any non-legalized return can mean being rearrested and detain by Immigration and Customs Enforcement (ICE), charged, sentenced and again deported.

Anyone with information regarding the above incident that would help in proving Adrian Small's innocence, please contact detectives at the 25th Precinct (212) 860-6511.

*Photos Courtesy of Lamont Whealton
and Sheila Harrison*

RICHARD ALLEN SIMMONS "FRITZ"

The Team

FRITZ

ACE   **CHUCKY**

SHEILA HARRISON

Age 10

WILHELMINA HARRISON
The Mother of Sheila, Junior, and TyRay

LEROY WALKER

Sheila's Stepfather and Pedophile

ELIZABETH & CLAUDE ROBINSON

The Grandparents

CLIFFORD "JUNIOR" HARRISON & GERVASE "TYRAY" WALKER

Fritz's Half-Brothers

CLIFFORD "JUNIOR"   **GERVASE "TYRAY"**

112ᵀᴴ STREET FAMILY

112ᵀᴴ STREET FAMILY

DARRYL HARRISON

Sunrise March 8, 1978 – Sunset July 29, 1979

Darryl Jr with his Sister, Nicole Harrison taken weeks before Darryl Jr.'s fatal fall from a 5th floor window.

Fritz's Neices And Nephews By Half-Sister Sheila Harrison

Young Neil, Raven, Nicole, and Howard

Adult Nicole, Neil, Raven, and Howard on Sheila's Wedding Day

Fritz 1ˢᵗ Memorial Celebration
December 9, 2016 At Angel Of Harlem

Harlem Holiday, Sheila Harrison, Freeway Rick Ross, and Fritz's Sister Evelyn Simmons

A Moment if Silence and a Toast to Richard "FRITZ" Simmon

LETTERS TO HEAVEN

My Dear Beloved Brother,

You left me too damn early. But I didn't have any say about you leaving, my brother. You were put in the hands of the Great Master.

Never forget my sweet brother, you were loved by your mother, children (Dominique Jean Morris-Simmons, Sequoyah Michael Simmons, Chance Allen Simmons, Richard Allen Simmons, Raymond DaJahn Simmons, Terry [R.I.P.], Mandy Williams, and Erin Anis Cunningham), your sisters, and brothers. We love you with all our heart, my kind, beloved brother.

Richard, you were a damn good man. You were a great son and brother, and the best father any child could ask for. You were selfless and gave your all to anyone who needed it. There was never malice or wickedness in your heart for anyone. If there were more people like you, it would be a better world.

You left an imprint on all our hearts that will last a lifetime and beyond. No one can replace you. I understand now that God didn't add another day in your life because he loved you and needed you more. My Brother, you will always be missed.

Love You Always, EVELYN

Dear Fritz,

First and foremost, I would like to say that it was a pleasure to know you and be a part of your life. The love you have given me is irreplaceable. The way you showed love to the people you cared about was uniquely your own. What am I supposed to do now that you are no longer here with me? The only thing left for me to do is continue to remembering you every day that I'm still living.

As for myself, I'm maintaining my composure as I journey through this maze called life without you and Chucky. Staying focused and sucker-free. When I heard that you had moved on to the other side, I really thought that you had faked your death to get away. I had to ask Evelyn to tell me the truth and when she did, my heart was torn to pieces. It took me many years to accept what happened to you. I was filled with hate after finding out a certain person did not do what I asked him to do to help you at a critical time in your life.

I am truly sorry that I was not there to protect you and care for you the way you needed. You were always there for me when I needed you, but I was not there for you. I hope you can find it in your heart to forgive me for not being there. Unconditional love is what you have given me from day one and I am grateful to have received it. You were my everything; my mentor, and friend but most of all my brother. I LOVE YOU FRITZ WITH ALL MY HEART ALWAYS, AND FOREVER, NO MATTER WHAT TILL DEATH.

Your loving brother,
Honor & Loyalty
ACE aka KING MARIO

Dear Fritz,

Wherever you may be, I pray that all is well. It's been over 25 years since you left us and you are still missed. You left an impact on Harlem that is still felt to this very day.

You would be very surprised at what has become of your beloved Harlem. Without sounding too prejudiced, you would not believe the large influx of white people who have moved into Harlem. Yes, you read that right. Along with our new neighbors came a makeover in parts of Harlem, so its appearance would shock you. Expensive condos are popping up all over the place, which we can't afford to live in. But what's most surprising is the sidewalk cafes, restaurants, and trendy bars that are lining the streets of Harlem. You would not recognize 8th Avenue (Frederick Douglass Boulevard) with white people are walking around Harlem late at night without a care in the world. Shocking, isn't it? But enough about that.

I want you to know how much I've missed you over the years. I will always cherish those early years when I met you as a teenager. Those were some of the best years of my life. Hanging out with you guys gave me confidence and brought me out of my shell since I was somewhat shy. Remember how we used to hang out at your house after school and play records. You guys taught me and my first girlfriend Sally how to hustle. That was huge, especially since you guys teased me because that girl walked off the dance floor on me because I couldn't hustle. I was taught well because I became one of the better dancers. Like the O'Jays song, "Living for the Weekend," that was us. We lived to party on weekends. We went all over partying, then you came up with the idea of charging admission. The way we promoted the parties and the large crowds that we drew, I think we would have been very successful as promoters if we had continued.

My memory of you is in two stages: The Fritz who liked to go to parties and dance. The second stage of our friendship was when you became a more serious person and became interested in the streets game. Our foursome had broken up by then. As you know I started coming around 112th more. I met Tojo and TyRay and a new foursome developed. Remember how Queen Bee taught us the ways of the game? You took those lessons and ran with them and you exceeded anything we could have imagined. You were always ambitious, ever since I could remember, always thinking of ways to make money. With your aggressive nature and ambition your rise was inevitable. It turned out to be a good thing though. You gave back to the community and your generous nature touched many. I'm glad to have had you in my life and I will never forget you. As a matter of fact, you won't let me. I say this because over the 25 years or so that you've been gone, I've dreamed about you many, many times, much more than even my own family. When I mention this to Evelyn she said, maybe you're trying to tell me something. I guess that's how much of an impact you have had on my life.

Well, I'm a married man now with a family, wish you could have been here for the wedding. I think you would like my wife; she keeps me in line, ha, ha, ha. My son is fascinated with you. Even though my family never got a chance to know you, they feel like they do because I have shared with them, my memories of you. Well that's all for now. Say hi to Carl for me.

Your Brother & Dear Friend Always,
DARRYL

Dear Fritz, My Brother from Another Mother.

Yes, I. did it. I'm finished. I'm done. Yes, there were times I wanted to give up and scrap the book because of the ridicule and attacks, the vicious slander and comments in the street and on social media. On this journey, you came to me, many times in my dreams, never threatening, and always smiling. I took it as a sign from Heaven that you were giving me your stamp of approval and co-signing this book, letting me know to keep focus, let nothing stop me, and keep writing.

I'm good Fritz. I'm a fighter, a survivor, with a tough skin. Your story is much bigger than the people who would love to stop it, keep you quiet, and buried. There is a young lady out there telling bits of your story, riding on your name, getting social media fame using unauthorized photos of you without consent from your family, and vowed that this book would never hit the streets, to that I say, "My God is a mighty God."

The deeper I dove into uncharted waters, the more I understood why they didn't want your story told. I refused to let that happen, to be bullied, or your sisters (Evelyn and Sheila) and friends (Ace, Big Gee, Chucky's son Charles, Chucky's common-law wife, Shelagh, Darryl, Gums, Karl, Kashmir, Lamont, Rambo, Ray, and Trick) be stopped from telling their truth. I am from the old-school. I play fair. I gave "everyone" the opportunity to share their memories of you, so no one person could say what's not the truth, or that I was being bias in writing this book. It took me a little over two years to write your story. Many believe that it was two years too long. The ones doing the talking never wrote a book. They are clueless about the discipline it takes to write a book. They do not understand the sacrifices I've made, my time, my energy, and my family. There are three types of books a writer can put out, good, mediocre, and bad. The Harlem Plug is my first non-fiction book, and I refuse to put my name on anything that is half-assed. I'd be doing you an injustice, myself, your family, and the readers.

The biggest misconception people have about writing a book is the finances involved. No, I didn't get paid upfront to write The Harlem Plug. It was a struggle and a financial hardship for me. I had to pay for the book's editors (a Developmental Editor, a Copy Editor, a Content/Line Editor, and a Proofreader); then there was the printing cost and the book promotions. I did have a financial partner, but she pulled out. She had other financial obligations more important than this book. So, I was left standing, holding the bag and an incomplete book in my hands. I had my faith and my God. I knew this setback was only temporary, because here we are reading your story.

It's been a helluva ride Fritz., you have touched the lives of many people, and have fans globally. I didn't realize how many people were interested in your story. I uploaded chapters 1-3 on Wattpad.com, and had well over 9,000 readers, becoming the No. 6 bestseller out of thousands of books listed on that site at the timed, I edited and posted my interview footage on YouTube, the subscribers on my channel (Author Harlem Holiday) are in the thousands, and the videos viewed are in the hundreds of thousands. I contribute the majority of that to the support of Kevin and Tiffany Chiles; publication and article I wrote on you for, Don Diva Magazine.

I hope you'll forgive me if there is anything you might have put differently. Please note, they can't sweep your story under the rug anymore. And, now, everyone knows you were more than the rumors they spread about your death, and the drugs you sold. They will never forget you, books never die, and when they are long gone, people will still be reading The Harlem Plug.

Peace My Brother. Your Sister,
HARLEM HOLIDAY

ABOUT THE AUTHOR

Tiffany Símone Fulton was born and raised in Harlem. She spent some time in the Highbridge section of the Bronx and found her Prince Charming in Brooklyn, where they courted and married a year later on Valentine's Day. She now writes under the pen name HARLEM HOLIDAY. Like the famous jazz singer, Billie Holiday, she acquired the signature flower above her ear, a style that symbolizes sophistication, glamour, and femininity.

Harlem Holiday has been writing short stories and poetry for over thirty-years, that she shared with family and her close friends. She went to Gotham Writers' Workshop to enhance her story writing skills. She attended an HBCU, Lincoln University in Pennsylvania where she pledged Alpha Kappa Alpha Sorority and briefly attended the New School where she studied film and screenwriting. On June 2, 1999, she graduated with a B.A. in Communications, Film, and Video from The City College of New York, where she was honored for Outstanding Leadership and Services as a Peer Academic Advisor, and 1st Prize recipient of the university's Civil City Project Award, for her poem, *The Melting Pot*. Because of the loss of a first cousin and the rise of HIV/AIDS among youth and women of color, she put her writing and film work aside to focus on the needs of the community. In 2008, she founded Silent Voices United, Inc., a not-for-profit 501c3 grassroots organization and was a full youth and young adult agency partner of the Riverside Church Global HIV/AIDS Ministry, under the Spiritual Outreach Services (S.O.S). For a couple of decades, Harlem Holiday has been on a crusade to educate communities of color disproportionately affected by HIV/ AIDS.

The alliances enabled Harlem Holiday to create and launch the widely recognized "Got Tested" peer to peer campaign started by her son Ronnie. She, along with her young adult peer educators could be found around the city wearing their signature black GOT TESTED? T-shirts, distributing HIV/AIDS materials. The campaign kicked-off in the Highbridge section of the Bronx and where over 300 residents were tested in one day. It was confirmed by Dr. Monica Sweeney, former Assistant Commissioner for New York City Department of Health and Mental Hygiene the Bureau of HIV/AIDS Prevention and Control, that the program tested over 3,000 youth throughout New York City the first year the campaign was launched. Her son, who was instrumental in starting the "Got Tested" movement, in 2011 received the Youth Distinguished Service Award of the New York State Dept. of Health AIDS Institute for his work.

Her approach was unique and yet simple. She used music and entertainment to promote HIV/AIDS awareness and safety, while educating, strengthening, and empowering underserved at-risk communities. In addition to joining the fight against HIV/AIDS, her passion to impact the quality of life in her community led her also to focus her organization's efforts to create opportunities to develop and empower young leaders. Through Silent Voices United, Inc. her leadership has encouraged a generation to participate in bettering their community through collective action, creating alliances and partnerships with various organizations with similar visions, developing programs that foster social change, and increase community access to corporate and private resources in health and social services.

In addition to her social work Harlem Holiday is the author of FALLEN PETALS: THE DECEPTION, THE DECEIT, & THE DAMNED, the first book in her *Fallen Petals* three-book series. It is a reflection of the bitter realities her work has allowed her to witness and fight in her life's journey.

If you enjoyed *The Harlem Plug* take a sneak peek of Harlem Holiday's crime novel

COMING SOON

FALLEN PETALS:
The Deception, The Deceit, And The Damned

HARLEM HOLIDAY's much-anticipated crime fiction novel takes readers on a roller-coaster ride through the life and mind of 17-year-old Symone Harris, a victim of a violent sexual assault at the hands of a predator Jack Fisher, her father's best friend and crooked partner in the NYPD.

This story unravels the beginning of Symone's dark, life-changing secret, the assault and subsequent pregnancy. The rape turns her life upside down. The embarrassment and guilt Symone felt, lowered her self-esteem and self-worth, which contributes to the poor choices she makes.

When Symone goes to extremes to conceal the truth from her family and friends, it has a domino effect. She spins a web of lies, trying to bury the dreadful secret of the rape and pregnancy, but instead everything spirals out of control. Ultimately, Symone's deceit causes many to suffer and destroys the lives of all those she loves, one at a time.

Symone must tell the truth, stop Detective Jack Fisher from hurting anyone else or lose everything, but will she do it before it's too late?

CHAPTER ONE

Lost Innocence

Jack Fisher, a borderline psychopath in his mid-thirties, average in size and looks, except for his clean-shaven pock-marked face, and a severe military crewcut. Jack is speeding eighty miles an hour into the night, his young travel companion asleep in the passenger seat. He reaches into the glove compartment of his Lincoln Continental, takes out a vintage flask, and swigs some of the vodka inside.

It's 1978 Symone Harris is nine years old, innocent and without a care in the world, as she lies in a peaceful slumber curled up with her doll. She wakes, sits up, yawns, and stretches.

"So, you're finally awake, sleeping beauty." Jack says, brushing her thick black hair out of her face.

"Yup." She nods. I wonder what time it is? We've been riding for hours, Symone thinks, yawning again.

She peers out of the window and sees that day has turned to night. The long empty highway is dark and eerie. To her, it looks like they are driving into a black hole.

Symone looks across to the driver's side window, then twists around to the rear window. There is complete darkness and no cars in sight. The only lights on the highway are from their car.

"Are we almost there?" she asks.

"No, we still have some ways to go. Take a sip of this and settle back," Jack says.

He hands her the flask and she drinks.

"Yuck!" Symone says coughing up the alcohol, then hands it back to him and tries to wipe the taste off her tongue with the end of her shirt. "What's that?"

Jack laughs. "Something to help you go back to sleep."

"I'm not sleepy, just tired of being in the car." I know Uncle Jack lives across the George Washington Bridge in New Jersey, but not so deep in the boondocks. They've been driving for hours. She thinks to herself.

Symone squirms from side to side to get comfortable. She's restless and unable to fall back to sleep. She grabs her dolly and gazes out of the glass moon roof. The sky is pitch black, which makes the stars sparkle more. They are bright and beautiful as they flicker in the clear night sky.

Symone searches for the Big Dipper. "A shooting Star!" she exclaims.

Jack grins and glances down at her. "You better hurry up and make that wish."

Symone shuts her eyes and wraps her arms tight around her dolly. "Star light, star bright, the first star I see tonight; I wish I may, I wish I might, have the wish I wish tonight." She exhales, opens her eyes, points to the clusters of stars and begins to count. "One, two, three…"

Jack exits the thruway.

Symone stops counting and sits up. She rolls down the window and sticks her head out. She inhales and catches a whiff of the summer night air. She claps her hands softly and wiggles her legs.

We're here. I can't wait until we get to the house. I'm tired of all this driving and my butt is starting to hurt.

SYMONE'S PARENTS, VAUGHN AND MAE Harris, both went to high school with Jack. Vaughn, almost the opposite in looks from Jack, is 6 ft 2, and has an athletic build. Although he is quite handsome, with smooth dark-chocolate skin, it's his, full lips and wide smile that first attracted Mae. Vaughn and Jack played on the football team. Mae was the captain of the high school cheerleading squad. Her long legs and shapely body proved to be a distraction to the whole team, but to Jack and Vaughn especially.

Jack had spent all of his young life bouncing around the foster care system where he was abused and neglected. At thirteen he moved to Jamaica, Queens, next door to Mae with his new foster parents. He had been found on a church step, wrapped in a blanket, with his umbilical cord still attached. He was left there, abandoned by his teenage mother. Jack's new home was in a predominately African-American community. The kids bullied and teased him, the only white kid living in the neighborhood, at the time. It didn't help that he was tall and lanky. His pale skin, and light blonde hair, and blue eyes, also didn't help him blend in. The neighborhood kids called him albino, Sasquatch, Bigfoot, white-boy and honkey. But Mae was always kind to him and would comfort him on the really bad days when he got jumped by the neighborhood bullies. She introduced Jack to Vaughn the captain of their high school football tea and the three became best friends. Vaughn got Jack to join the football team and Jack, put on muscle, and toughened up. Once he started fighting back, he gained his confidence and the respect of the neighborhood boys, who also knew that if they messed with Jack, they were also messing with Vaughn.

Symone loves when he comes to visit her parents because of all the attention he gives her. She calls him Uncle Jack and thinks of him as her second Dad. She's known him her whole life. He always brings gifts when he visits, which is often; flowers for Mae, and toys and dolls for Symone.

It was the weekend of Vaughn and Mae's tenth anniversary. Jack stopped by the house to bring them anniversary gifts. He gave Mae a bouquet of daffodils and expensive sapphire earrings and Vaughn a case of Cohiba Cuban cigars and a bottle of whisky.

"You've outdone yourself, Jack. How can you afford all this on a rookie's salary?" Mae asked.

"Price is no object when it comes to friends," he laughed. Vaughn popped open the bottle, and he and Jack sat, drank, laughed and talked about "back in the day."

"So, what y'all doing for your anniversary?" Jack asked.

"We were going to the Poconos for the weekend, but Mae's mother got sick and can't watch Symone," Vaughn said.

"I'll take Symone with me for the weekend. I have off from work," Jack offered.

"Are you sure it won't be an inconvenience?" Vaughn asked. "You're a bachelor. You may not be ready to babysit a nine year old." "What are friends for? Y'all go have a good time and enjoy your anniversary."

"Yay!" Symone yelled, running down the stairs, where she'd been listening to their conversation. She then jumped into her father's arms and smothered him with kisses. "You the best. Love you so much daddy."

"You better," Vaughn said, then reached into his pockets, pulled out a small black velvet box and opened it. Inside is a pair of heart-shaped opal earrings. Symone's birthstone.

"Daddy, they're beautiful and so sparkly." "Consider it the first of your early birthday gifts."

"I love you Daddy," Symone said giving him a big hug.

Jack reaches behind him and pulls out a black Raggedy Ann doll. "Wow Uncle Jack, Daddy couldn't find a black one for me. Thank you so much! You're the best god-daddy ever!" She jumped out of

Vaughn's lap and hugged Jack.

Mae appeared in the doorway of the kitchen. "Miss, aren't you supposed to be sleeping? It's past your bedtime."

Symone hurried over and kissed Mae on the cheek and gave her a tight hug. "I love you Mommy." She then skipped her way back into her bedroom with her dolly anticipating a wonderful weekend with her godfather.

"How far to the house now, Uncle Jack?" Symone asks.

Jack rubs and blinks his eyes, stretches and yawns. "We'll be there soon, but I need to pull over. I'm exhausted."

They pull into a small motel parking lot and park behind a long row of evergreen shrubs.

"I'll be right back," Jack says. He gets out, walks around the shrubs, and disappears.

Symone doesn't question where he is headed, nor is she afraid to be left alone in the car. In the distance, she can see a Disney movie playing in a drive-in theater. She watches it until Jack returns.

Minutes later, Jack gets back in the car with a motel key in his hand.

"I need a quick nap before getting back on the road. I don't want to fall asleep behind the wheel."

Jack drives to the back of the dimly lit motel parking lot, where there are several ground floor units. He helps Symone out of the car and they walk up to a door, which he unlocks with the key. Symone plops on the bed and looks around. It's a small dreary unit. There is a mirror above a shabby dresser with an outdated television in front of the queen-sized bed.

Jack turns on the television. "I'ma watch the news. There's clean towels and soap in the bathroom. You should take a shower."

We must still have a long way to go if I have to wash up, Symone thinks, then she shrugs.

"Okay."

Symone goes into the bathroom, removes her clothes, pulls back the glass sliding door, and gets in. She turns on the water, and it feels good on her skin after the long ride. She closes her eyes, stands under the shower head, and imagines she's in a sprinkler. A few minutes go by, the sliding shower door opens and a cool breeze hits her back. She opens her eyes and Jack is standing there naked with a washcloth and soap. She looks at him and twists up her face. What's he doing in here? She turns away and pretends he is not there, until he starts to wash her backside, then between her legs. Her body tenses up. Eww, I don't like this.

Symone is numb as she presses herself against the tiles away from Jack. She can't speak or move. Her brain seems to have temporarily shut down. When she opens her mouth, she is unable to articulate her words clearly and begins to stutter. "I... I ah... I'm ready t-t-to g-g-get out n-n-now."

"I'm not finished," Jack says.

"I... I'm f-f-finished," she whispers.

To prevent Symone for panicking, screaming, and attracting attention, Jack steps aside, allowing her to leave.

Symone moves as close to the shower wall as possible to avoid touching Jack. When she tries to slide the door open; it's stuck. She tugs on the handle a few times. It doesn't open. She tugs back and forth and grits her teeth. She starts to shake. Her chest tightens, and her breathing is rapid. She feels faint, her legs are giving out. "Take it easy, I'll open it."

"O-k-k-kay."

Symone exhales and nods, but does not look at her godfather. How can she ever look at him the same way again? She grabs a bath towel, covers herself and hurries out of the bathroom. In the bedroom she looks at her reflection in the mirror. She stands there for a long time before she takes off the towel and hurriedly dries herself. She scrubs her face vigorously, her neck, and then her arms. She rubs her entire body, trying to wipe away the feel of her godfather's hands.

Symone is back home with her parents after the weekend with Jack. She is traumatized, not the same nine-year-old girl who left. She didn't tell her parents about what happened because she didn't know how.

A week after the incident, Symone's in the park with her friends playing hopscotch. After that they play several games of jacks and then tag on the monkey bars. The sun is hot and the music from the Mister Softee truck can be heard coming down the block.

"Last one to the ice cream truck is a rotten egg," Zoe says. They jump off the monkey bars and race to the corner.

"Symone's the rotten egg." The girls point, tease, and laugh at her. "N-nuh-uh. I'm not a rotten egg. Y'all th-the rotten egg." "Who's the rotten egg? Symone's the rotten egg!" they chant.

After the incident with Jack, Symone is ashamed and extra sensitive. She no longer wants ice cream. She fans the girls off, turns around, and heads back into the park.

"Hey, where you goin'? Don't you want an ice cream cone?" Zoe asks.

Symone shakes her head.

The girls pay the ice cream man and run to catch up with Symone.

Denise puts her arms around Symone's shoulder. "We were just playin'. Why you gettin' mad?"

"You been acting funny lately," Zoe says. "You okay, Symone?" "If I tell y'all s-s-somethin' . . . y'all p-promise never to t-tell anyone."

Zoe makes a cross over her heart. "Cross my heart and hope to die, stick a needle in my eye."

Symone and Zoe wait for Denise to promise. She grabs Symone's hand, entwining their pinkies. "I pinky swear."

The girls walk back to the park and sit on the swings. Symone pushes herself slowly back and forth. Her eyes are fixed on the ground as she speaks.

"L-last weekend… my d-daddy's f-friend t-touched me…" "Touched you?" Denise says, frowning.

"Yeah, t-t-touched me…d-d-down there." Symone points between her legs.

The sounds of children laughing in the park, dogs barking, and pigeons cooing all fade into the background. Symone has a far-off look in her eyes as the girls wait for her to continue. But no matter how much her friends question her, she doesn't say another word.

Days after she tells Denise and Zoe about the incident, Symone distances herself. Vaughan and Mae notice a change in her behavior and are concerned when she refuses her friends' visits and calls. She now spends most of her days in her room, staring off into space.

Mae knocks on Symone's bedroom door then walks in.

"Denise and Zoe are outside and want you to go to the park with them."

"Not today. It's too hot."

"It's beautiful out. Are you okay, baby?" Mae asks, as she feels Symone's head and cheeks, checking for a temperature.

"Yes." "You sure?"

"Yes, Mommy."

Mae gently kisses her forehead then leaves. When Symone is sure the door is closed by the click of the latch springing into place, she grabs the dolls and stuffed animals on the bed and tears them apart, one by one, starting with the Raggedy Ann.

FALLEN PETALS:
The Deception, The Deceit, And The Damned

Print / eBook /Audiobook
COMING SOON ONLINE @
HarlemWestsidePublishing.com
Worldwide, Amazon, and Barnes & Noble

FIND ME

Author Harlem Holiday

Facebook:

Wattpad:

YouTube:

Instagram:

Twitter:

Linkedin:

Pinterest:

Tumblr:

Website:

www.ingramcontent.com/pod-product-compliance
Lightning Source LLC
Chambersburg PA
CBHW070915030426
42336CB00014BA/2423